Moving Fast
on the Slow Track
Strategies for Career Success

Moving Fast on the Slow Track

Strategies for Career Success

ENID A. GOLDBERG

Scott, Foresman and Company
Glenview, Illinois   London

ISBN 0-673-18087-5

Copyright © 1986 Scott, Foresman and Company.
All Rights Reserved.
Printed in the United States of America.

Library of Congress Cataloging-in-Publication Data
Goldberg, Enid A.
  Moving fast on the slow track.
  1. Job hunting.   2. Success in business.
I. Title
HF5382.7.G65   1986   650.1′4   85-24972
ISBN 0-673-18087-5

1 2 3 4 5 6–RRC–90 89 88 87 86 85

This book is dedicated with love
to Allan and our parents,
Rose and Morton and Rita and Milton,
to our children, Daniel and Elizabeth,
and to Silky – who is dedicated.

Table of Contents

Acknowledgments

Many thanks go to Kathy Pickering for her careful typing of this manuscript. Thanks, also, to John Wendland and Ron Zemke for their thoughtful previews and excellent suggestions; and to all the editors I worked with at Scott, Foresman for their help and encouragement.

Moving Fast
on the Slow Track
Strategies for Career Success

Introduction

Have you ever thought, at one time or another, that you were moving too slowly on your career path? And have you ever wondered if you were on the right track in the first place? Like most people, when considering a career in the business world, you may think in terms of the obvious, big-money-making "line" jobs: accounting, trading, financial analysis, bank lending, investment banking, account management, product development, sales. If you don't feel suited—through personality, skills, or background—to these types of careers, or if you aren't selected for these professions, you may feel you are getting off to a bad start. Many people go through an entire lifelong career in an area they consider "slow track," never recognizing the opportunities this career path offers. And if they do get a job on a "fast track," they may stay in the job even if they are unhappy because they do not know other professional areas exist. Or they may be perfectly suited to the fast track, but still need guidance as to how to maximize their opportunities and move rapidly ahead.

If you are one of these people, this book is for you. It is for you if you are seeking professional success. It is for you if you want to explore and do well on a career path other than a standard MBA track, and it is for you regardless of which track you are on if you want to make the most of the opportunities you have.

The first part of the book deals with various "staff support"— or "service"—areas (corporate communications, human resources, administration, systems, marketing support, etc.), and describes the kinds of jobs and career opportunities that exist there. There are also chapters on how to match yourself to a

career path in which you can succeed, and how to prepare yourself for entering the job market. There is some practical advice
on getting and keeping jobs, learning how to make the most of
your innate skills, and discovering how to acquire those you
weren't born with.

A particularly important section of the book deals with strategies for getting ahead—in "staff" areas or in any other line of
work—and points out the pitfalls along the way and how best to
avoid them.

There is much to learn in this book about yourself. There are
discussions of failure, as well as success, and tips on what to
do if you see in yourself some of the personal weaknesses the
book describes.

In the final analysis, this book is for everyone who cares
about his or her career and wants to do well in it. Drawing on a
vast body of research and experience, the book attempts to
prepare you for succeeding in one of the most important aspects of your life—your career.

Part I
Staff Work

Chapter 1
Fast Track/
Slow Track

Everyone knows about the fast track. It's populated by young, dynamic corporate executives with finely honed quantitative and analytical skills; with aggressive, but preppy, personalities; and with "success" writ bold on their horoscopes. They fill the training programs at major banks, aspire to impressive account management positions at prestigious investment firms, and anticipate accruing millions trading options and futures.

"Line" jobs are usually considered "fast track." They are the jobs in areas that earn income for a company. In banks, the line jobs are the lending officers' jobs; in insurance firms, the salespeople are on the line; in computer software companies, those doing line work are inventing and selling the programs. Line jobs, if done successfully, bring money into a business; they are concerned, really, with the making and selling of a product.

But what about the other track—the one that business school wisdom says is slow and dull and vulnerable to budget cuts? The one described in embarrassment as "staff," instead of proclaimed proudly as "line"?

"Staff" really means support jobs. Staff people in corporations perform functions that don't actually bring in money, but that businesses can't do without. Support staff people work behind the scenes, lending assistance in service areas such as marketing or running computers. They are in human resources departments and recruit and train people, draw up salary plans, or decide what kind of people the company will hire in the future. They are in communications and deal with press releases or write corporate newsletters. They run the building in which a corporation is housed, or plan menus, or provide accounting or legal services. They award corporate grants or handle a company's advertising strategy.

The staff positions discussed in this book are those on the professional level, where certain skills (varying from job to job) are prerequisite to attaining a specific position. Among professional positions, staff jobs can be at a variety of levels, from entry level to senior executive level. And, contrary to what many people believe, plenty of staff employees get far up the corporate ladder, even though on the surface they seem to be working where the action isn't.

The slow track is important in corporations. MBA schools frequently downplay course studies in staff areas, but they do offer such programs. Companies often don't recruit actively to populate this track, but they do hire for it. In fact, they generally have no trouble culling stacks of resumes from a well-placed ad in a large newspaper—resumes not only from people already in other staff jobs or aspiring to find a service position, but from the disenchanted in other "high-powered" fields as well.

An example or two will illustrate this point. Martin Kingston answered an ad when he completed an advanced degree in English literature, and found himself transported from the edge of the groves of academe to the corridor outside the corporate board room—at a threefold increase in salary over his last "job," which consisted of teaching a composition course here, filling a one-year part-time administrative slot there, and indexing a full professor's book for university press publication somewhere else. The rewards of such peripatetic scholarly pursuits in an overcrowded field—and Martin was one of the lucky ones who actually found employment—did not seem worth the years of disciplined and specialized study it took to earn the degree. Rare, indeed, were the positions teaching the vagaries of Joyce or the influence on the epic of the Norman Conquest to enthusiastic and receptive English majors. When full-time positions were available, they were usually wholly or in part teaching English as a second language or instructing in remedial composition—for one- to three-year nonrenewable contracts, and often for salaries that would have caused any self-respecting municipal sanitation workers' union to strike.

Martin answered an ad, beat out the dozens of other corporate hopefuls in a series of interviews and written evaluations, and landed the $25,000 officer-entry-level position at a major financial institution in Boston. His job was to construct a communications module for the credit officers' training program. This meant developing a course to teach bright and articulate fast-trackers destined for success on the line how to organize their ideas, write them down, and present them out loud; and then to do the actual teaching. No easy task for a "staff" person to accomplish among "line" people whose salaries and rank equalled his own. But, with the memory of his four-digit academic salary nipping at his heels, Martin plunged in.

Although his initial knowledge of the commercial banking industry was limited to what he had digested from a few textbooks and scattered annual reports, he talked to people and read widely during his first few months on the job to fill in the gaps in his financial knowledge, and he drew heavily on his background as a teacher and student of writing to construct a thorough and useful program for the training course.

His next step, to implement the program, was more difficult. Winning the confidence of people with MBAs, who often had a built-in disdain for the humanities, required special interpersonal skills—also known as "tact." Again Martin drew on his resources as a humanist and teacher. He freely admitted to his class his rudimentary knowledge of and admiration for the banking industry, but he showed a quiet classroom-bred confidence in his own areas of expertise—writing and presentation skills—that would not be outshone by any MBA glitter. His success was helped, too, by the juxtaposition of Martin's training module with the trainees' first scheduled written and oral presentation, a lesson Martin remembered: the easiest things to succeed at are the things that are really needed.

Now Martin's module is an established part of the training curriculum, and his job has expanded. He hires others to teach the module, travels to bank locations in other parts of the world to set up similar programs, and is working on an expansion of his original module to make it applicable to senior officer-level skills-development programs as well. His "slow track" staff job—three years down the road—has netted him two promotions, a considerable raise, and an additional yearly bonus, with the next few levels of advancement clearly defined.

Taking the puck toward the goal hasn't been without its checks, however. There were moments when Martin felt he was being crushed against the boards. The style of the corporation, for example, conflicted with his background and experience. Getting used to (and affording) a blue-suit wardrobe was the easy part. Shifting from an arts-oriented, intellectual environment to a blue-suit mentality was more difficult. He was puzzled by what he perceived as decisions based only on cursory and not very in-depth analysis; he was angered by the interminable delays he suffered in getting projects through the approval process; and, at the times of his greatest frustration, he longed for the "meaningful" work he had left behind—shaping young minds and delving into complicated academic or literary issues.

But his armor and face mask held, and these lapses became less frequent as he discovered not only kindred personalities, but similar backgrounds among his cohorts. As his real understanding of the business world increased, he also came to appreciate and respect aspects of economics hitherto beyond his reach. Instead of looking backward, he focused on the career path in front of him, and felt more and more comfortable with his surroundings as he began to climb the corporate ladder and make rewarding and interesting contacts with others in his new world.

Most staff jobs, of course, don't require advanced academic degrees. At the other end of the academic scale, Tom Mercato, with a fresh B.A. in journalism and "experience" consisting only of writing and editorial work on his college newspaper and a summer job in the packing area of a local department store, also answered an ad, which turned out to have been placed in a Chicago newspaper by a headhunter. The position it described was an entry-level public relations job at a midwestern food corporation. The job paid only $17,000, but offered an opportunity to learn the public relations business from the ground up.

Tom's first assignments consisted of checking facts for other people's press releases, assembling press kits, and typing. He often felt frustration and anger at some of the more menial things he did between 8:30 and 6:00, when he came early and left late to get his work done. But he was realistic enough to know that he had to establish a track record and gain some credentials before letting go of a salary-producing job in his chosen field, regardless of its level. He was twenty-one, as yet unencumbered by family responsibilities, and determined to hang around until he moved ahead.

Things moved very slowly for Tom, however. A recession was underway, inhibiting corporate expansion; attrition didn't appear to be taking place at a great rate; and movement upward seemed illusory. In addition, the attitude of Tom's fellow workers toward him was negative. They—including Tom's boss—saw him as an arrogant and not terribly talented hack, and repeatedly passed him over for promotion to the few higher places that became available. But fortune and Tom's own initiative worked in his favor. A hiring freeze eventually made it necessary for all members of the PR staff to expand their responsibilities, and ingratiating himself with the editor of the in-house publication soon made it possible for Tom to do some writing. A year and a half later, with his portfolio a bit fatter, Tom went back to the headhunter who had placed him initially and landed another position, this time with a small marketing firm that needed someone to develop and edit a newsletter reflecting trends in the food business.

The job was replete with difficulties, since some members of the company's senior management weren't convinced of the need for such a publication and would only fund the project at a low level. Tom took the job at a salary increase of only $2000, but he recognized the opportunity to work an area from the ground up. What his former colleagues took for arrogance served him as a sense of confidence when he suddenly found himself on his own, expected to demonstrate his ingenuity and skills. There were inherent risks, but the challenge of proving himself outweighed any reservations for Tom.

Now, two years later, Tom's publication is widely acclaimed in his firm. He has a staff of three and intends to expand his publicaiton list to include a four-color quarterly report and a biweekly marketing report. His salary has also begun to grow and the headhunter is calling him now.

Jobs like Martin's and Tom's—and there are many such positions in staff support areas—represent a hidden miniority in the business world, but a sizable and very real series of career paths. Making the decision to enter the corporate world in the first place takes a lot of thought. If the career choice you make *is* in the corporate world, a staff job might be right for you.

This book will depict some of the professional directions staff jobs can take, annotate the successes—and the failures—of those in various service fields, advise about beginning and successfully staying on staff tracks, and discuss where these avenues may lead.

Chapter 2
Service Areas

Staff jobs are called service jobs or support jobs for a good reason: those who hold them provide services that help those whose business it is to increase the bottom line, but the people performing these services do not bring in earnings themselves. Many staff functions could, theoretically, be handled by a line employee—and they often are, particularly in small companies. However, delegating these functions to staff professionals who can do them quickly and efficiently often yields better finished results, and leaves the line employee free to concentrate his or her efforts on doing business.

Not all companies are wealthy enough in people or in dollars to afford this luxury; it is primarily large corporations that can pay employees to specialize in such arcane professions as "internal communications" or "manpower planning." But there are enough companies in this category—especially in large cities—to create a myriad of career paths; and even small companies often hire a communications and marketing expert or a human resources professional to handle any and all tasks relating to those fields.

The kinds of staff areas you might find in a corporation can be most easily explained by referring to the organization chart shown in Figure 2-1.

The opportunities depicted on the chart can be categorized as follows:

- Jobs relating to the physical running of the organization (the maintenance and security of the building;

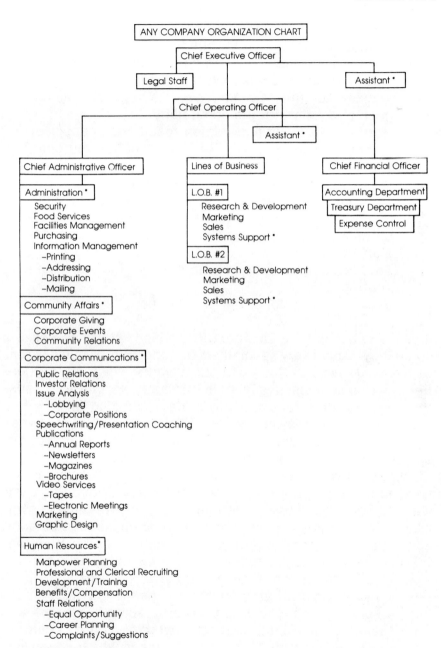

ANY COMPANY ORGANIZATION CHART

Chief Executive Officer

Legal Staff

Assistant *

Chief Operating Officer

Assistant *

Chief Administrative Officer

Administration *
  Security
  Food Services
  Facilities Management
  Purchasing
  Information Management
    –Printing
    –Addressing
    –Distribution
    –Mailing
Community Affairs *
  Corporate Giving
  Corporate Events
  Community Relations
Corporate Communications *
  Public Relations
  Investor Relations
  Issue Analysis
    –Lobbying
    –Corporate Positions
  Speechwriting/Presentation Coaching
  Publications
    –Annual Reports
    –Newsletters
    –Magazines
    –Brochures
  Video Services
    –Tapes
    –Electronic Meetings
  Marketing
  Graphic Design
Human Resources *
  Manpower Planning
  Professional and Clerical Recruiting
  Development/Training
  Benefits/Compensation
  Staff Relations
    –Equal Opportunity
    –Career Planning
    –Complaints/Suggestions

Lines of Business

L.O.B. #1
  Research & Development
  Marketing
  Sales
  Systems Support *

L.O.B. #2
  Research & Development
  Marketing
  Sales
  Systems Support *

Chief Financial Officer

Accounting Department
Treasury Department
Expense Control

Indicates Staff Opportunities

FIGURE 2-1 **Staff Opportunities**

the provision of food; purchasing responsibilities; mailing and internal distribution)
- Functions dealing with the community at large (corporate giving; special events, many of which are planned for the community or clients; establishing good relations with the community)
- Positions in managing human resources (manpower planning; recruiting and training; benefits and compensation; staff relations)
- Work in communications (public relations; investor relations; issues analysis; speech writing and coaching; writing for publications; preparing videotapes; organizing meetings and seminars; advertising; design work)
- Aide-de-camp positions attached to high-level executives
- Systems jobs supporting line groups

(Legal and accounting jobs are often called "staff" as well, but since they require very specialized training, and because no one can enter these positions without advanced degrees in these fields, we will not discuss them in this book. Nor will we discuss the many existing research positions—including financial research—because they are so varied that it would be hard to categorize them. It should be noted, however, that research of one sort or another often accompanies many jobs.)

This chart represents general functions. Not all companies have all these functions, and not all organize them in the same way. Some companies handle these functions through centralized departments as shown above, and some companies allow each line of business to hire people to perform staff functions for its area. While many large corporations today have centralized support functions, a recent trend is to streamline businesses by having staff areas report to line managers. In applying for specific jobs, you will have to do some homework and find out (through annual reports, word-of-mouth, business library reference material) how companies in which you are interested are organized. In the remainder of this chapter we will discuss these areas in detail.

ADMINISTRATION

Often overlooked as an area in which to work, administration offers opportunity for advancement within a firm in jobs requiring good people skills and a lot of common sense. Although many people working in administrative areas—security, food services, building management, purchasing, and information distribution—are hired as unskilled laborers, the managers of these areas are often hired at more advanced levels. Though some managers rise from within the ranks, others are hired from outside.

Meredith Katz, for example, graduated from college without knowing what field she would enter. She had spent some time studying home economics, although this had not been her major, and she decided she liked working with food enough to consider that preference in looking for a job. She was neither a dietitian nor a cook, but she figured that there had to be room on the management side of corporate food operations to accommodate a bright person willing to work her way up. She was right. She applied to the professional personnel areas of several commercial banks in her locale. (Large commercial banks are noted for their generosity in subsidizing food services for their employees.) One of the recruiters was so surprised at the specific nature of her request that he granted her an interview. She landed a job as assistant to the coordinator of dining facilities at a bank, and was very pleased with the variety of work her position entailed and with the people she met on the job. While her initial position was not a very high-level job, her boss's was; and when he left the company a few years later, Meredith succeeded him.

There are additional areas of opportunity in administration other than food services. Managing the security and maintenance forces in corporations also offers openings for people who are good at organizing others and monitoring their activities. In addition, managing large printing, distribution, mailing, and addressing operations offers challenges and opportunities for those whose interests lie in this direction.

The field of purchasing has its own demands. Business school graduates who studied merchandising are often hired for jobs in this area; but companies also look for purchasing managers with a more general background—people who know value and have taste, who can manage budgets, who can learn how to filter through the complicated world of wholesale buying, and who are scrupulously honest.

Administration managers rarely have the flexibility to get out of their departments and into the structure of the corporation at large, but many such employees are very satisfied with the career paths open within their departments.

COMMUNITY AFFAIRS

Most corporations feel a sense of responsibility to the outside community. As a result, many companies have special staffs that are knowledgeable about education, art, theater, health care, and other nonprofit areas. These people make decisions about the company's charitable contributions. These employees often have had experience in the education, art, or health world before deciding on a corporate career, and this experience can be invaluable to a business involved in making choices and value judgments about proper recipients of corporate support.

Not only do corporations give away money, but they frequently feel an obligation to be a good neighbor in their community and undertake projects to improve their area. They might, therefore, have need for a special staff to organize and implement these activities. For example, the businesses in the Wall Street area in New York City have an association dedicated to community improvement. The association, through grants from these businesses, supports art exhibits in the area, sponsors clean-up campaigns, underwrites free outdoor concerts and dance programs, and generates good will in the area. Many of the Wall Street firms that are participants in this association have employees whose partial or entire responsibility is in fostering and supporting these activities.

Another related function is sponsoring and orchestrating special corporate events. These can be parties or sports events for customers, benefit evenings for a community group, gatherings of various industry representatives, or meetings and seminars for people within the corporation. These events require much planning and it is necessary to have large staffs to handle everything from invitations to after-dinner speakers. Often, nothing more than pleasant personality, intelligence, and an ability to organize are sought as prerequisites for these jobs.

Like their administration equivalents, most special events and community affairs jobs do not often lead to anything outside their departments. These positions do, however, afford excellent opportunities for meeting people and making contacts, and they can be very exciting jobs.

COMMUNICATIONS

"Everyone communicates every day, so why pay people to do it professionally?" This question is common among detractors of communications as a field, particularly during an economic recession. But the sad truth is that not all professional people in the business world today are capable of composing a coherent position paper, writing or presenting a speech, lobbying in Congress, dealing with the press, or preparing an annual report. And those who *can* do so, frequently don't have the time to do so. Thus: corporate communications departments. The importance of this field has been recognized by prominent management experts. John Naisbitt, in *Megatrends,* says, "The new source of power is not money in the hands of a few, but information in the hands of many."[1] Thomas J. Peters and Robert H. Waterman, Jr., authors of *In Search of Excellence,* say, "the intensity of communications is unmistakable in the excellent companies."[2]

Communications can be divided into two categories: external and internal. External communications covers a wider range of activities than internal in most companies. The targeted audience of external communications activities consists of individuals or groups outside the corporation. These external ac-

[1]John Naisbitt, *Megatrends* (New York: Warner Books, 1982), p. 16.
[2]Thomas J. Peters and Robert H. Waterman, Jr., *In Search of Excellence* (New York: Harper & Row, 1982), p. 122.

tivities include dealing with the press—knowing whom to talk with, when, what to say and how to say it, and what image the company wishes to project. Press relations is a major preoccupation of many companies, since a company's public image often affects its sales and stock performance. External communications also encompasses interaction with investors, community groups, and federal, state, and local government bodies.

External communicators are really salespeople and policy advocates. They promote a company's good name. The bigger the company, the more the services of external communicators are needed. In addition, speechwriting—the art of researching and writing policy and position statements for high-level corporate executives in words they might have chosen themselves—is often a major task in external communications departments.

Also considered as an external communications responsibility in many corporations is marketing support—the preparation, production, and distribution of material geared to promote and sell a company's products. Such material might include brochures, flyers, slide/sound shows, and videotapes.

An area related to marketing is advertising. A company's marketing strategy frequently calls for an ad campaign, and while independent advertising agencies are generally hired to write ads and place them in the media, a company needs a staff of its own to work with the ad agency to ensure that the company's marketing goals are met, to help the agency maintain a consistent image for the company in the ads, and to oversee the work and make sure it is done on time and within the company's budget.

Corporate advertising people and advertising agency people often switch back and forth, but corporate advertising also is open to those with other experience in the corporation or other experience in communications. This area is fast-paced, is filled with interesting contact and travel opportunities, and although it may not lead to the very top of a corporation, is often rewarding and satisfying in its own right.

Internal communications, really necessary only in large corporations, helps employees talk to each other—to those further up the corporate ladder; to those on lower rungs; and to those at the same level but in different departments. Such communications might be accomplished through publications—newsletters, magazines, memos, and position papers; or through presentations, speeches, or slide or video shows. Internal communications departments also frequently maintain resource centers or reference libraries as well.

Some communications areas are both internal and external. "Issues analysis," for example, spans both. Issues analysts are often specialists in history or government, who also know a lot about the industry in which they work. Their job is to analyze legal, governmental, or business situations in which a corporation finds itself, and to define the company's point of view on those situations. An issues person often functions as a lobbyist, representing his or her company's interests in Washington, in a state capital, or in a local government. In conjunction with the company's senior management, the issues analyst prepares position papers for release to the press, or to state the company's position publicly to employees or to the community at large. For example, the legal changes currently affecting the banking industry are making it essential for banks to articulate their positions on these topics to their employees and to the public. Some specialization is necessary for jobs in this area, but an issues person does not have to have a business or a communications background.

The most cogent reason for a corporate communications group is to support a company's profits—to provide services that help line areas do their jobs better and more efficiently. Thus, a publication assisting cross-selling of the products of several departments by carrying information essential to the sales force is more valuable to a corporation than a newsletter listing retirements and ads for used cars, however popular the latter might be with some employees. And a publication deemed necessary to doing business is less likely to be cut during a budget crunch.

Communications departments tend to attract people with generalist interests, but very specific skills: writing and editing talents; slide, graphic, and video production knowledge; public speaking and persuasion know-how (and the ability to get along with and command the respect of others); and the ability to quickly comprehend and distill large bodies of new and frequently unfamiliar information.

Such people can often be found among the ranks of humanities majors—people who would, ironically, often find themselves unemployable or underpaid if they chose to look for employment in the overcrowded arenas of journalism, publishing, or higher education, their traditional stomping grounds.

For example, it took Paul Claude until he was twenty-eight to realize that his college ambition to be a newspaper reporter, stemming from his days as a student journalist, was attainable only at great personal cost. Landing a job as a reporter for a small-town weekly—a position that allowed him a certain amount of freedom to schedule his own time and write about what he felt was important—paid him considerably less than what he needed to support his growing family.

So, portfolio in hand, Paul followed the advice of a family friend and answered ads in newspapers and professional journals for corporate writers. He accepted an entry-level public relations job at a large financial services firm in New York, writing releases and placing articles in the press.

Being on the other side of the fence felt awkward for Paul at first, particularly because he was dealing every day with people whose jobs were similar to his old position. But the writing skills he had developed as a reporter were crucial to his present responsibilities, and the immediate $10,000 pay increase (with more expected) did a lot to soothe his injured ambitions. Working for a corporation, espousing corporate views and promoting corporate positions, instead of writing what he thought was "vital" and "provocative" was something that Paul learned to accept. And, in fact, he soon found that he was beginning to enjoy being a corporate communicator.

Corporate communications used to produce only printed material, but recently, videotapes—and to a lesser degree 35-mm slides, including those generated by computer—have been used increasingly as vehicles of communication. In-house video groups—especially those in multinational corporations—are taking on the preparation and circulation of tapes of important meetings or speeches within their corporations; some are even preparing internal news programs about their organizations for their staffs. As technology advances, video units are used to electronically "hook" together corporate meeting rooms around the world so that a company meeting in

Chicago, for example, can appear on a screen in London, and vice versa. In addition, new advancements in videoconferencing allow participants in different locations not only to see each other, but to talk back and forth. Using slides to provide illustrations during a talk is an excellent way to make a point stick in the mind of your audience.

For anyone with audio or video training, the area of corporate communications will offer increasing opportunities in the future. Most communications departments also have artists and designers, who do the graphic work that accompanies the print material.

Being a company communicator may appear to some the equivalent of being a "corporate mouthpiece," but those in the field have often experienced the satisfaction of knowing that their professional contribution has helped turn a troubled company around by changing its public image, or has helped boost corporate morale, or has increased business through a well-placed advertising campaign. For example, a financially troubled corporation in a major city recently, through good press relations, avoided having its dirty linen aired in public while it tried to regain its economic balance. In addition to its efforts with the press, the company was frank and optimistic with its employees to keep morale up during the crisis. The effort was a success. Morale remained high and the company's public image didn't suffer. When the crisis was over, the company could focus on profitability again with a renewed sense of cohesiveness and self-respect.

Though positions in communications usually exist only at companies large enough to afford the luxury of hiring writers and promoters, the functions of a communications department can be extremely significant to these companies.

HUMAN RESOURCES

The most populous staff track is human resources, formerly known as personnel. While many years ago this area focused primarily on hiring nonprofessional employees, today's human resource staffers cover a wide variety of duties, including salary and benefits administration, training and development, corporate headhunting, college recruiting, and employee relations. Many of these activities have become so specialized that they are now major subjects in business schools.

Perhaps nowhere have human resources activities become as specialized as in recruiting. In many companies there are executive, professional, and clerical recruiters—in-house "headhunters"—who perform both reactively, screening applicants for a variety of jobs, and proactively, seeking out candidates to fill select positions and assisting in the manpower planning decisions of the company. Moreover, as was pointed out in a recent cover story in *Business Week*,[3] corporate strategic planning is increasingly a function of business line groups, and is no longer done only at the top levels of a company. Therefore, human resource manpower planners are more and more frequently finding themselves part of a line-of-business team, contributing their personal know-how to the long-range, as well as the everyday, workings of their company.

While it is true that business schools offer courses in staff specialization areas, many recruiters have little formal training in their area when they begin their careers. They are generalists by trade: people with liberal arts backgrounds and very good interpersonal skills. Indeed, the art of talking, listening, and knowing how to make a person feel comfortable (or uncomfortable) are the stock-in-trade of recruiters.

Corporate recruiters cull their applicants from college campuses, where they speak to or interview undergraduate or business school students; from responses to ads placed in various publications; from personal contacts in other companies; from professional headhunting firms (often for a large fee); and from stacks of unsolicited resumes directed to "Personnel Manager, XYZ Co." They at times stoop to pirating by offering golden handcuffs to attractive potential candidates. Once in a while headhunting firms even pirate the same person more than once, by calling back a successful placement with a better offer after a discreet period of time.

To some, the word "recruiter" connotes a glib slickness,

[3]"The New Strategic Planner," *Business Week,* 17 September, 1984.

tempered by insincerity. While this reputation is not wholly undeserved, recruiters, by and large, are committed to doing the best for their company by attracting as many good people as they can find. Their role is central to a well-run corporation, and it is a very viable career path for a person with a nonspecialized background who is a good judge of character.

Those wishing to land a position as a recruiter can begin at various levels, depending on the degree of information and background they have about the line of business in which the company to which they are applying specializes, and depending on their people skills. A novice may begin by interviewing and hiring keypunch operators or cafeteria workers; a "corporate" type with experience in the company's line of business may find him or herself hiring managers.

A less plentiful but equally important personnel type is the manpower planner. This type of position is rarely entry-level. A manpower planning specialist often has extensive experience in other areas of personnel, and perhaps even an MBA in the area. He or she knows the company's line of business well and works with the company's senior management in making manpower plans and projections. This profession represents a very viable human resources career path. Every company moves in certain directions, and the most successful businesses foresee their hiring needs and begin early to identify positions and fill them.

Another related human resources activity is training and development. Professionals in this field run orientation programs, or impart knowledge to a company's most ambitious or promising personnel about everything from management techniques to business writing. Often, these training jobs require knowledge of a certain set of skills—expertise in presenting an oral report, for instance—as well as knowledge of a product or business service.

Still other human resources career paths involve specialization in salary and benefits planning and administration; and human resource career paths can also lead to concentration on employee relations areas such as affirmative action, counseling, employee activities, or employee suggestion systems.

People with liberal arts or generalist backgrounds can

prepare for entry into these areas by completing an MBA program with a specialty in human resources management or organizational behavior. It is also possible to work one's way into certain human resources career paths by starting at the bottom, in entry-level jobs, with a B.A. However, this is becoming less and less true, especially in areas such as employee relations and compensation and benefits.

An example will illustrate how being in the right place at the right time can also help someone begin a career in human resources. Take the case of Sandra Wolpath. After earning a teaching and psychology degree at a southern college, and several special licenses, she found a low-paying, part-time, non-secure position as a guidance counselor in a big inner-city school system rife with budget constraints and terror in the hallways. The job market in her area was tough, and she was one of the "lucky" ones to be working right after graduation. After five months, Sandra was mugged in the parking lot of her school. She handed in her resignation the following day.

Sandra lived with a married sister for three months while she searched the want-ad pages of the newspapers, contacted placement agencies, and blanketed the city's business district with her resume. However, letter after letter remained unanswered, and she was on the verge of reapplying to the Board of Education when she bumped into a college classmate who was working in sales in an insurance firm. The friend talked her company's professional-placement officer into interviewing Sandra. This was all the break she needed. Although on paper Sandra's credentials looked like those of many other young women in their early twenties, in person Sandra came across as sophisticated, articulate, and competent.

She had no experience relevant to the main business of the firm—selling insurance—but her energetic and professional personality impressed the recruiter and Sandra was asked to return for another series of interviews. This time, Sandra, who was black, met with the head of human resources, who informed her that the company wanted to begin a program to recruit minority students for their training program. Not only did they feel Sandra would be able to put such students at ease, but

Sandra's intelligence, confident personality, and corporate appearance would help her serve as a role model for other minority-group members.

Sandra enjoyed three years as a recruiter for the insurance company, learning about other areas of human resources as well, and was then hired away by a commercial bank to head up an affirmative-action program designed to help the company meet government guidelines on minority hiring practices.

Sandra had doubled her teaching salary when she joined the insurance firm; when she was hired by the commercial bank they increased it 25 percent more. While human resources jobs have never been considered high paying, particularly since they are salaries, not commissions, pay scales in many firms are very respectable—certainly the equivalent of positions in other staff areas.

All human resources jobs do not have the same potential for advancement, either in the department or in the firm as a whole. At the top of the list are tracks in employee and industrial relations, and in compensation and benefits. People in these areas often attain power and influence with senior line managers in a corporation, and often move into line jobs themselves. More dead-ended jobs are usually training and development positions, which tend to be low-visibility slots. Those filling these positions are not generally involved in strategic planning or large-scale budget planning activities, but very often find their jobs satisfying nonetheless.

SYSTEMS SUPPORT

A far more technical staff area than human resources and communications is systems support. This is a burgeoning field for professionals today, as office after office—in major corporations and small firms alike—becomes automated, and as more and more information is put on-line. Computer skills—developing and maintaining programs, assessing office needs, devising automated ways to meet these needs, and being conversant with the computers themselves, both to work and repair them—are now as essential to a well-run and efficient operation in most businesses as familiarity with the telephone was half a century ago.

Most high-level positions require specially trained professionals, often with graduate degrees in engineering, but, because of the relative newness of the field, there are often opportunities that involve on-the-job training or offer training courses as part of the package. And opportunities seem to be unlmited for those who keep up with technological advances.

Many major commercial banks in large cities, for example, maintain both an entire corporatewide systems department to explore and develop computer support of business, and individual mini-systems in each department. Thus, major projects as well as minor ones can receive the benefit of systems technology; and bankwide applications as well as specific applications can be developed.

Automating an office—or a corporation—also results in jobs other than ones relating directly to the computer. How office space is to be used—space planning—is an important consideration, for example, when new technology is brought in; people have to be hired to deal with the physical rearrangements and psychological ramifications of such a move.

Because the field is so new, people can sometimes move into systems career paths with nonstandard training. When Joseph Willoughby, for example, was studying literature at an Ivy League university ten years ago, he fancied himself destined for a career in humanities research and teaching. His senior thesis, however, involved learning to use the computer to categorize certain types of information quickly and retrieve it when necessary, a skill that changed his life. When he graduated with a B.A., fully intending to pursue a doctorate in his chosen area, his advisor pointed out the difficulties of finding work in an overcrowded field, the low pay scale, and the probability that Joe would wind up teaching courses in fields such as composition and English as a foreign language, when eighteenth-century poetry was his specialty.

Joe reconsidered and went to graduate school in systems management, receiving a masters degree and finally a doctorate. He was accepted in the degree program because he had learned a reasonable amount of computer lore in conjunction with his thesis research. Today Joe heads one of the divisions of the systems department mentioned above, and although he has twinges of regret now and then when he thinks of the ivory tower or the joy derived from educating young minds, his current job provides a strong career path, stability, a salary which enables him to live in a comfortable suburban community with his family, and time enough to enjoy it.

Salary, in fact, is a very real motivation for many people to enter systems. Because so many new systems applications are being discovered all the time, and because the systems field is not yet glutted, companies are often willing to pay systems professionals higher salaries than people with equivalent experience and education in other areas. Moreover, to enter systems fields one doesn't have to be a mathematical wizard. Strong analytical and reasoning skills and some quantitative ability are really all it takes to begin to learn computer skills.

INDIVIDUAL STAFF JOBS

Sometimes staff support positions are not part of any department at all, but are individual jobs in various parts of an organization. For example, some people become special assistants to senior executives—not administrative assistants, but high-level and well-paid professional assistants who really help a senior executive perform his or her function.

It takes a special kind of personality to want to be what has been called a "horseholder." A horseholder is an assistant to a corporation president or high-level official: a speech writer, an aide-de-camp, a personal liaison with the outside world, or a buffer. Depending on the type of firm to which the horseholder belongs, he or she may do everything from making major decisions to dealing with the press, from writing a policy address to handling complaints addressed to his boss from other company employees. If you are the kind of individual who enjoys basking in the reflection of other people's sunshine, or who is willing to learn the business thoroughly in this way, the rewards are many.

Horseholders earn a lot, are privy to important information and policy decisions, wield power as a result of having the ear of a prime mover, and often see their ideas and suggestions implemented. Such people must be articulate (both orally and in writing), composed, intelligent, presentable, and quick to rebound from setbacks. A keen sense of the business in which their boss engages and strong analytical skills are necessary, too. Many such people are realistic enough to recognize that they do not have the skills or background necessary to become the president themselves, and are content to sit next to the throne, making their own not-inconsiderable contribution.

One such "assistant-to" was Ryan Brill. He consciously decided on such a course when he found himself passed over several times for line jobs in a pharmaceutical firm. Though he knew the product line well, and though his background was in marketing and communications, he was not selected to lead sales teams or to run promotional campaigns or to lobby for the industry in Washington. Nor did he fit in as a researcher, since he held only an undergraduate degree in chemistry, not the Ph.D. necessary for drug research.

But Ryan had strengths of his own. He was personable and well liked by everybody; he knew many people in the industry; he wrote and spoke well; and he was quick and bright. Most of all, he got along well with and was a personal friend of the president of the company. The two men had been college classmates and had entered the firm at the same time; and although the president's career had been more stellar than Ryan's, they had remained close. Furthermore, Ryan was secure enough not to envy his friend. He was the ideal candidate for the job of the president's special assistant, and both he and the company benefited by the liaison.

Assistant-to positions are not always at the late end of a career path. Horseholder positions are often seen by ambitious young movers as ideal first jobs. Despite the "go-fer" overtones such positions have, they can be stepping-stones to executive positions (such as division manager) and other jobs either not available through normal promotional channels, or available through such channels only after a long climb. A talented employee, if successful as a young horseholder, can move up very quickly in a corporation, placing himself or herself in a position to achieve a top management job at an impressively early age.

Another special assistant, Elvira Connelly, exemplifies this point. She worked for the head of a small but financially strong ad agency. Elvira was considerably younger than her employer and they did not start out as personal friends, but the latter was impressed with Elvira's energy and intelligence and saw the special-assistant position as good experience for a person with the potential to go far in the advertising field. Elvira did indeed go far, actually taking over the agency's management when her boss retired eight years later.

The rewards for this type of individual staff position can indeed be large, but so can the risks. Although Elvira's position turned out to be the opportunity of a lifetime, Ryan's boss was fired by the board of directors eighteen months after Ryan got his job, and Ryan lost his job as well. The new president wanted his own right-hand assistant, and Ryan was too much identified with the discredited policies of the departing executive to have an independent career path at the firm. Things did not turn out too badly for Ryan, however. Losing his job forced him into the job market, and because of his experience as a horseholder and the knowledge of the industry he gained from this job, he got the line marketing job he had always wanted at another firm.

The need for individual staff jobs can be found in most large corporations and even many small firms that do not have staff support units. These jobs are frequently hard to come by because of their uniqueness, and they are often filled from within the ranks of a company because knowledge of the company is necessary to do the job. But at times an executive search firm will be employed to find a candidate for the position and the job will be filled from outside the corporation.

The above descriptions of various staff jobs give you a general idea of the career opportunities you can find in service areas. These jobs are often overlooked by many seeking to enter the business world, but they offer the chance for rewarding and satisfying work and should be carefully explored if you are not set on pursuing a line job.

The word "rewarding" brings up another point. While job satisfaction and security are important rewards for finding a job that is a good match for you, finding a job at a satisfactory salary is also important. Too many people feel staff jobs are chronically underpaid, both at entry level and at the most advanced levels. While this may have been true at one point, and while it may be true to some extent today in certain companies, the earnings gap between line and staff for most jobs is narrowing, especially in large corporations that value their staff departments. *Training and Development Journal,*[4] a human resources publication, reported that as a general rule, the more employees in the organization, the higher the income in a staff area. The journal was referring to human resources training jobs in particular, but the same observation applies to other staff areas as well. The article categorized most jobs it surveyed as being in the salary range of $30,000 to $40,000, with beginning positions and jobs requiring little experience being in the $20,000s. Communications jobs, as listed in communications trade publications, compare well with human resources jobs in this respect, and recruiters place other staff salaries in the same range. The most-senior-level jobs in staff departments do of course pay considerably higher, but more factors are involved in setting these levels, so no generalizations can be made.

No generalizations will hold entirely true, either, about the kinds of people who are attracted to staff jobs. However, the kind of person most likely to be attracted to and succeed in most areas in the staff world is the generalist—a well-educated person with a wide range of skills and interests. John Naisbitt, in *Megatrends,* says, "We are moving from the specialist who is soon obsolete to the generalist who can adapt."[5]

The staff world offers opportunities for generalists of all types—for those most interested in people to those most interested in machines; from those interested in managing large

[4]Steven Langer, "Compensation in Training and Development: An Update," *Training and Development Journal* 37, no. 5 (1983): 50 ff.; and Steven Langer, "Compensation in Training and Development: An Update," *Training and Development Journal* 39, no. 3 (1985): 27 ff.

[5]Naisbitt, p. 37.

staffs to those interested in implementing others' decisions; from those whose principal concern is invitations and food to those who think only long-range strategic planning is a worthwhile activity. The range of challenges is broad, and so is the scope of staff activities. In the next chapter, we will consider where these kinds of opportunities can be found.

Chapter 3
Where the Jobs Are
. . . and What
They're Like

Staff jobs exist in any size corporation or business, but they are most frequently found in large corporations, where greater specialization occurs in both line and staff areas, and where extra funds are usually available to support staff jobs. Such positions are in either centralized staff departments or within line departments.

Jobs similar to those in staff departments can also be found in consulting firms specializing in these services. These jobs are considered "line jobs" in small firms where the line of business is, for example, communications or professional placement. While you may initially choose—or be chosen for— a large company or a small firm to begin your career, it is not necessary to commit yourself exclusively to one or the other. Part of your flexibility in a staff job is that you can move back and forth.

For example, Alicia Petrovsky's career spanned both worlds— the large corporation and the small, specialized firm. She started her professional life after college in an entry-level position as a writer of press releases for a midwestern insurance firm. She wrote short news items presenting her company's stand on internal developments and public issues, basing her writing on material gleaned directly from the chairman's office. She also accrued a list of press contacts because she was required to place these press releases in local and national newspapers. The job was interesting, varied and meaty, but the pay was low.

So, portfolio in hand, Alicia used her vacation to journey to the big city—in this case Chicago—to sell her wares. Using the web of press contacts she had established through her first job, she networked her way into various public relations consulting firms. Although she didn't land a position immediately, one of her initial contacts paid off and after several more trips to Chicago she was employed by one of these PR firms, doing exactly what she had done for the corporation, but for nearly double the salary. The firm's clients included insurance firms like the one Alicia had just left, and her expertise was immediately useful.

Alicia's small-firm success only lasted two years. Recessionary repercussions caused setbacks in the PR firm's client base, and Alicia found herself not only out of a job, but unable to land another similar job because of the recession. She had some savings, however, and decided to risk hanging out a shingle and starting her own free-lance consulting firm, doing what she did best—writing for the press. At first, even with all her old contacts, the free-lance jobs she got were few and small. But she persisted, largely through necessity, and as the economy recovered and her portfolio grew, her contacts multiplied and so did her assignments. The story's happy ending is that Alicia now earns enough money yearly not to worry if a month or so goes by without an assignment; and the anxiety she occasionally feels at these times is more than compensated for by the freedom and creativity her free-lance work offers.

Going where the opportunities are—sensing growth areas and not being afraid to follow your instincts—is a good way to stay on top of a career in the staff world. This means not limiting yourself to either a large corporation or a small firm as a professional environment.

Other considerations when you are assessing opportunities in the job market are geographic location and industry type. At any given time, some areas of the country are growth areas and some are not; and certain types of industries are healthier than others. A recent study of human resources training jobs in *Training and Development Journal* indicated that big cities, such as New York, San Francisco/Oakland, and Chicago, pay the highest median salaries, while the lowest salaries are found outside major metropolitan areas. The highest-paid industries are manufacturing, petroleum, chemicals, and pharmaceuticals; with communications services firms also paying respectable salaries. The lowest-paying tend to be banks and other financial institutions and health-related institutions.[1]

Going where the opportunities are—researching growth areas and not being reluctant to relocate geographically—is a good way to stay on top of a career in the staff world. This means not limiting yourself to a large corporation or small firm, an urban or rural location, or a specific industry as a professional environment. Be as flexible as possible.

POSITIONS TO AVOID

A mistake easy to make in taking a staff job—especially your first such position—is falling into a dead-end clerical slot. While all clerical jobs are staff jobs, not all staff jobs are clerical. Staff jobs—like line jobs—often have seemingly menial tasks associated with them, but clerical jobs are primarily menial and rarely provide opportunity for creativity or growth. While it is possible to begin a job in a clerical capacity and achieve promotions through good performance, such advances are the exception, not the rule.

Carrie Paul found herself in a dead-end job. A liberal arts college graduate with a major in political science, Carrie took a first job as a typist/receptionist in a human resources consulting firm in Atlanta. The interviewer stressed the interesting

[1]Steven Langer, "Compensation in Training and Development: An Update," *Training and Development Journal* 37, no. 5 (1983): 50 ff.; and Steven Langer, "Compensation in Training and Development: An Update," *Training and Development Journal* 39, no. 3 (1985): 27 ff.

tasks and career opportunities the job offered. She pointed out that the last person who had held the job had been promoted to assistant account executive in less than a year. (What she failed to tell Carrie was that her predecessor was a cousin of one of the firm's vice presidents.)

When Carrie began her job, her day was filled with phone messages and typing—not writing—memos. After four months, the story was the same. No interesting tasks were visible on the horizon. The managers she worked for treated Carrie curtly, and clearly had no intention of giving her any responsibility. Moreover, they weren't even pleased with her work. Although she maintained her good disposition, professional demeanor, and willingness to work hard throughout her stay at the firm, her typing skills were below those of those office workers whose training had been secretarial. Carrie's efforts to find a better job were stymied by the fact that she had been at her job only a short time and had no other experience. Moreover, potential employers classified her as a clerical. Although Carrie's situation was, in part, her employer's fault—they hired her under false pretenses—it was, nonetheless, Carrie who suffered.

With her heart set on a business career, Carrie stuck it out for a year and a half. She lived at home and saved her meager salary for tuition for an MBA program, then quit and entered business school.

First positions don't all wind up as dead-end slots. Edna Birkut, for example, took a job right out of college as a secretary for a small insurance firm and within fifteen months had been promoted to office manager. Two years later, she went into sales for the same company and today she is a vice president of the firm.

Edna and Carrie are not identical, of course; Carrie's personality is not as strong as Edna's. But luck has something to do with their different stories. Edna worked for more broadminded and imaginative people than did Carrie, and the firm she joined was in an expansionary mode.

Individual determination and talent, as well as being in the right place at the right time, contribute to how well you can do in a certain situation. It pays to think about all the alternatives when you are considering a career path, especially a career path in a staff area. Take a first job as a clerical after other opportunities have been explored, and only if you are young enough to put in a few years waiting for an opportunity to move—either up, or out!

THE "BACK-OFFICE" ENVIRONMENT

Service jobs used to be categorized as "back-office," and in many firms, they still quite literally are. Operations areas, systems sections, human resources departments (except executive recruiting areas), and communications departments (except public relation areas) have often been housed in less-than-posh quarters for the simple reason that these people have had little customer contact, and there has been, consequently, little reason to spend excessive sums on a lavish environment.

While this situation is not true in the small service firms whose clients must visit the office, it is true enough in many large companies—though not all—and should be a factor in your decision about whether to choose a staff career or a line job. The traditional back-office environment can have a demoralizing effect on staff personnel, especially if it is accompanied by low salaries and sparse career opportunities. Many companies have remained content to foster an atmosphere of second-class citizenship among their support employees.

In the headquarters of several large financial services companies, for example, the computer and operating staff walk on linoleum in subterranean, windowless caverns, while their line colleagues on upper floors walk on thick carpets and look out floor-to-ceiling windows. The personnel area of at least one major big-city department store is situated in an inner corridor, windowless, overheated beneath bare steam pipes, and dark enough to give even a casual visitor a headache.

However, things are changing. Many companies have begun to recognize that productivity is not high among demoralized staff, and have sought to upgrade the environment along with other aspects of staff jobs. Moreover, many staff areas have begun to deal with outside clients in their work. For example, many operations and systems departments now market their products directly to customers, and the production areas—as well as the marketing areas—consequently have had to upgrade their physical plants because clients frequently want to see where the particular process they are buying is taking place. And certain companies have begun to recognize that even when a service area is dealing with internal "clients," they are often high-level people in the organization, and a nonprofessional environment decreases the credibility of the staff area.

Sometimes the contrast between line and staff isn't very noticeable. In one commerical bank, for example, the corporate communications area is carpeted and has windows and plants. The only difference between the staff and the line area, in fact, is the color and depth of the carpet—brown and flat for staff, rust and plush for line. A subtle distinction, and not one which seems to bother most people in the department.

A more bothersome distinction for many staff members is being located outside corporate headquarters, or placed in an area away from the "doing business" floors of a corporation. Morale is low in one support department—the administrative department—at a large New York corporation because those responsible for the maintenance of the corporation's primary location are, themselves, housed in a smaller, older building a block away.

Corporations that favor such distinctions do so primarily for budgetary reasons. But the bottom line seems far away when one has to walk to another building to eat in the cafeteria, especially in the rain, or visits a colleague in the same company whose rank is the same, but whose office is three times as large.

Those sorts of differences may not bother you; but if they do, you may not want to pursue a staff career. Or, you may want to take another look at your own set of values. Are you sifting out the most important aspects of the job you are considering? Does a bigger office necessarily mean a better job? Are the long-range prospects of a job tied to the physical trappings? Some jobs begin modestly, but are the start of a solid and far-reaching career, and in addition, are intrinsically interesting. Other jobs may seem fairly impressive because of some immediate glitter, but do not really lead anywhere or comprise meaningful functions. It is important to carefully assess what a particular job is and where it leads; and it is important to be honest with yourself about what matters to you. *Your* bottom line on this issue should be whether such environmental distinctions matter to you. If they do, choose your company with care.

Another factor perhaps even more important than physical surroundings is a consideration of the demands made by various kinds of staff jobs. Although some staff jobs can be done in one place during fairly regular hours, the time/place demands of others are far more stringent and unpredictable.

Regularity of location and hours is, to a large degree, dependent on whether you are working for a firm with outside or inside clients. If you work for a consulting firm—human resources, communications, management, etc.—whose client base is other companies or individuals, it will be part of your job to visit the clients to discuss projects, to entertain them—even after working hours—when they are in your locale, and to drop everything else and work all night if they advance a deadline. If a consulting firm is unwilling to provide this kind of service, clients will take their business elsewhere.

If you have a position in such a firm, you are more likely to "live" your job than if you work for a large corporation where you serve a specialized function for others in your company. While you may still work long hours to meet emergency deadlines, and while you may still have some travel (especially if your company has more than one location), most staff jobs in large corporations tend to have reasonably predictable hours and locations.

Another environmental factor you should take into account is who your fellow workers are. A common myth among line employees at many corporations is that the staff areas attract the less dynamic portion of the work force. Peter Drucker, in fact, says that because service areas are not paid for satisfying customers, and because they have no competition, they do not perform as well as line areas:

> The one basic difference between a service institution
> and a business is the way the service institution is paid.

Businesses (other than monopolies) are paid for satisfying the customer. They are paid only when they produce
what the customer wants and what he is willing to exchange
his purchasing power for. Satisfaction of the customer is,
therefore, the basis for assuring performance and results in
a business.

Service institutions, by contrast, are typically paid out of
a budget allocation. This means that they are not paid for
what taxpayer and customer mean by results and performance. Their revenues are allocated from a general revenue
stream which is not tied to what they are doing but obtained
by tax, levy, or tribute.

This is as true for the service institution within a business
as it is, for instance, for the public school. The typical staff
department is not being paid for its results. It is, as a rule,
not even paid according to the extent to which its customers, that is, the managers, use it. It is being paid—in
many cases inevitably so—out of an overhead allocation,
that is, out of a budget. The fact that the service institution
within a business tends to exhibit the same characteristics
and to indulge in the same behavior as service institutions
in the public sector indicates that it is not business that
makes the difference. It is the mode of payment.[2]

Although Drucker's remarks are certainly true of some companies, at other companies staff areas *are* held accountable for
their own productivity, and their jobs are indispensable to the
line areas that produce income for the company. Moreover,
these staff groups know that if they don't produce, individuals
will be replaced, or the function they serve will be handed over
to an outside consulting firm.

The quality of staff personnel is as variable as the quality of
staff management or the strength of the job market. There are
movers and there is dead wood, and there are mainstreamers
and a variety of subtypes. While no one kind of person is attracted to staff areas, the skills required for certain staff jobs
often determine the type of person who will populate a given
field.

[2]Peter F. Drucker, *Management: Tasks, Responsibilities, Practices* (New
York: Harper & Row, 1974), p. 141.

It's important to find out as much as possible about your future fellow workers before you actually begin a job or even consider a field. It is helpful to know not only what kinds of jobs there are (so you can determine whether your skills would be of use in these jobs), but what kinds of people there are (so you can attempt to determine whether you'd fit in).

To begin to gather first-hand information about various jobs— where they are, what they're like, who else is doing them—draw up a list of everyone you know who has a staff job in an area such as one of those listed in chapter 2. Begin your own job network by contacting the people on this list and scheduling meetings—at their convenience—to discuss what they do, how they came to be doing it, and what it's like. Identify the purpose of your call right away: tell them you are seeking information about the field they are in because you have an interest in seeking employment in that area. (Most people are quite receptive when they know that all you want is information, and they are often flattered that someone else might be interested in pursuing the same career path.)

If you don't know anyone in a staff job, contact anyone you know (a relative, a friend, a friend's friend) in any business job and ask them for contacts in interesting staff areas. Don't be afraid to introduce yourself to a stranger as a friend of a friend of theirs. Chances are they'll be cordial, but if they aren't, call the next name on your list. Remember, you haven't lost anything but the price of a phone call, and you may gain some helpful information about a possible career path.

And look through major newspaper want-ads—both for specific jobs and for ideas about different fields. If you don't understand what a job is, go to a business library and look it up. Be proactive in learning about various fields and jobs. No one else will do it for you. Once you have given careful consideration to the kinds of work and environment offered by staff fields, you can focus your efforts on the job application process.

Part II
Match-Making

Chapter 4
Finding the
Right Job

Most people find themselves assessing the job market—for staff or line jobs—right after college or business school; for a variety of reasons others do so in midcareer. Whether you are looking for your first job or your ultimate job, your thinking process should reflect a lot of the same considerations.

ENTRY LEVEL

"Entry level" is usually thought of as the first step in a professional business career. ("Professional" or "official" jobs, as distinct from "clerical" jobs, are the ones most likely to be on a far-reaching career path.) It is, of course, the best of all possible worlds to find your "right" job and career path on your first try, but it doesn't always work out that way. However, for your first job, you should not be deterred from accepting an offer because you don't think it's perfect. It makes sense to take a job—even if it isn't what you really want—just to get your foot in the door. Once in an organization, you can look around. You can get to know an area or organization; talk to others, find out what they do; read trade magazines or professional journals; and map out a career strategy for yourself. Meanwhile, you are gaining experience and you are also making contacts who might be valuable when you begin another job search. Moreover, it is far easier to land another job—the job you really want—if you already have a job and are doing well at it than it would be if you were unemployed. Recruiters find people who are in demand much more appealing than those who aren't.

Don't worry about how long you've been on that first job, either. It is routine in the business world to keep the first job for a year or two, to get your feet wet, then if it isn't exactly what you want, to look around for another.

HAVE FOCUS

If you are just starting off, you should concentrate your attention on a defined area to pursue as a career path. Then you can turn your attention to developing the strategy you need to get on track. "Focus" is a crucial word. Recruiting annals abound with stories of vague, unfocused job hunters who assume that interviewers are going to look at their resumes and decide in which area or position they would best fit. In actuality, most interviewers reject such candidates out of hand. The most impressive applicants know exactly what kind of job they want, and in which industry. Moreover, they can verbalize just how their own skills and experience make them a good fit for these jobs. Even if interviewers do not have immediate openings for focused applicants, they are more likely to keep these candidates' resumes on file than those of unfocused applicants.

Several examples illustrate this point. Marty Landes, for instance, was a smart college graduate who majored in English. He decided to enter the business world, and since he had worked on his college newspaper and had done well in his English courses, he thought he might look for a job that had to do with writing. On the other hand, he had been president of his college fraternity and felt he was very good with people, so it occurred to him that working with others—interviewing them, perhaps— might be the kind of work he would enjoy. And yet, he reasoned, he enjoyed travel—he had spent his junior year abroad—and knew several languages, so maybe a job having to do with foreign countries would be exciting. And, not to sell himself short, he was really pretty good with numbers. He had almost been a math major. Marty, unfortunately, projected all of these feelings when he went to several on-campus recruiting interviews at his school. The business recruiters, trained to distinguish the focused from the fence sitters, rejected Marty because they felt he really didn't know what he wanted to do when he grew up. As in fact, he didn't. What he actually wound up doing was taking a clerical job at a brokerage firm, hating it, and returning to school for an MBA. By the time he had finished his advanced business degree, he knew exactly what he wanted to do, and he had some real skills to offer employers as well.

In contrast, Adele Wagner *was* focused when she graduated from college. She had always enjoyed logistical problems. Her fascination with this area extended from the mundane (she liked moving furniture around) to the academic (her favorite subject was geometry). She knew very few people in the corporate world, but she assumed that big corporations had to have people who planned out their space needs. After college, Adele didn't have enough money for graduate school, but she thought that if she could get into a space-planning department, she could begin architectural school part-time and eventually carve out a career in this area. Although most of the college recruiters Adele talked with on her campus were not recruiting for space-planning jobs, several of them were so impressed with the definitiveness of her goals that they arranged interviews for her with appropriate people in their companies, and before long Adele had several offers from which to choose.

A more typical case than Adele's was Tom Bernard's. Tom, who had majored in history, liked dealing with people and decided to begin a career in human resources. He applied for and got a job at a bank as a campus recruiter, reasoning that even though he knew very little about banking, he could at least relate well to current undergraduates. Simultaneously, Tom begin a part-time graduate business degree (paid for by his company) which combined banking courses and human resources courses. His career was off to a very focused start.

ASSESS YOUR SKILLS AND GOALS

Before you begin your job hunt, do your own self-assessment. Analyze your own strengths and weaknesses and try to determine where you will be most productive: in which kinds of jobs, in which kinds of fields, in which types of environments, working with which types of people.

Begin the search process within yourself. Carefully consider questions such as why you want to enter a specific job market; what type of job you really want, and in what kind of surroundings; what your near- and far-term goals are and whether the jobs you are pursuing will help you achieve these goals; and whether the bottom-line considerations (salary, vacation, travel requirements, relocation requirements, benefits) meet your needs.

Before doing anything in the way of contacting people or companies, sit down with a piece of paper and a complete afternoon, and write out what you think are your strong points, weak points, needs and desires. Determine your goals and plan your strategy. Discuss your answers with your spouse, an understanding parent, or the "right" friend (one who isn't too opinionated to hear what you're saying, and one who is perceptive enough to cut through the surface of your remarks to what's underneath). College placement officers and counselors can serve this purpose, too, and so can a good headhunter. But in the final analysis, the most valuable counselor for you is you, especially if you can be honest with yourself.

Determine what your real strengths are. And don't forget about your specific needs and weak points. Try to determine whether you have interpersonal skills, analytical skills, quantitative skills, technical skills, language skills, managerial skills, or teaching skills. What these words really mean in the workplace, and whether you have these skills (or need them for any given job) should be a vital part of your self-assessment.

INTERPERSONAL SKILLS

The term "interpersonal skills" means the ability to get along with other people—above you, at your level, below you—in the workplace. It also means the ability to smooth ruffled feathers, to get people to do what you want them to do, to make them accept the fact that you might not always do what they want you to do, and to make others respect you enough to enable you to get your job done. It does not mean making everybody like you.

It means having tact and the ability to sense nuances. It

means knowing when to assert yourself and when to bow out; when to give up and when to give in; when to argue and when to acquiesce. It means understanding the needs of others and making them aware of your own needs without offending them. It means, in many cases, getting along with someone you don't respect or like.

The easiest way to acquire interpersonal skills is to be born with them. The second-easiest way is to observe and emulate those who always seem to keep their cool and get what they want. Notice how they react to certain situations, then try to determine whether you would have acted the same way. Though tact, discretion, and good judgment are hard to learn, if you follow certain rules, you will be making a good start:

- Hold your tongue, especially when angry or upset. Much that is said in haste is better left unsaid. People tend not to forget an insult or a diatribe, and even if it only happens once, they tend to think of such an outburst as a chronic character flaw. If you are angry or upset, wait until you calm down and think through a situation before you react to it.
- Keep your cool. Don't reveal how bothered or puzzled you really are, and avoid reactions that you will later regret. Assess each crisis situation calmly.
- Never put anything into writing in haste. If you react to a situation with an abusive memo, for example, you will not only look uncollected and rash, but after the incident blows over, there will be a permanent record of your response. Worse yet, if you have misinterpreted a situation, or if your reaction is just plain wrong, your written response will undoubtedly find its way into a mounting file of evidence that can be used against you.
- Avoid gossip. Those who gossip with you will turn around and gossip against you at the next lunch or coffee break. Most gossip is vicious and nonproductive, and those who remain above it generally gain respect. It certainly does not do your reputation any good to be cited as a source of gossip. Conversely,

avoid giving anyone information that can be used as gossip about you.

- Similarly, eschew rumors. Don't start or repeat rumors, and don't believe those you hear. Although there may often be some truth to rumors, as there can be to gossip, such information is usually useless professionally and does more harm than good to both the subject of the rumor and the spreader of it.
- Avoid comparing your present experiences and colleagues with those you have known in the past. Such comparisons only annoy others, and while you should certainly assimilate and learn from your past, you will stagnate if you try to live in it.
- Avoid *ad hominum* arguments. If a project is bad, label the project, not the creator of it. The less personal the complaint or criticism, the easier it is to overcome and get back to business as usual.
- Resist ascribing blame unless the accusations are proven and the consequences of ascribing blame are carefully considered. Few people are magnanimous enough to forgive someone who has blamed them for something they didn't do, so think before you accuse.
- Respect others—whether they are equals, subordinates, or superiors. Notice their good points, not only their flaws, and make them aware that you are doing so.

All jobs require interpersonal skills. Even the most back-office staff worker has to get along with fellow workers, bosses, secretaries, clients, or vendors. A person with a straightforward manner, an engaging smile, and appropriate dress, who looks you in the eye and appears uncomplicated and easy-going will generally land—and keep—a job much more easily than someone who is perceived as being devious, critical, unduly convoluted, grumpy, iconoclastic, or snobbish.

One specific way you as a staff employee can use interpersonal skills is to be a "make-things-happen" back-office person. You can become a favorite of people in, say, sales positions, who need the support of a service group. If you make sure the sales and marketing people know that *you* know how important the client is and that you not only want them to succeed with the client, but will help them to do so, your credibility will increase—with the sales and marketing people, with their management, and ultimately, with your own boss. In addition, don't hesitate to give other people public pats on the back: send their boss a note, praise them to others, praise them to their face. You'll be surprised to find how many of them will return the favor.

ANALYTICAL SKILLS

"Analytical skills" are problem-solving abilities. These skills are a combination of logic, reasoning, and just plain common sense. Having analytical skills involves the ability to

- Look at a problem and determine probable causes and logical courses of action to solve it.
- Synthesize large quantities of material and draw conclusions.
- Retain a body of knowledge and base suggestions for improving a situation on past experience.
- Think up new approaches to old problems.
- See problems in context, not as isolated events.

While all jobs require some problem-solving ability and judgment, the most responsible jobs frequently require the strongest analytical skills.

Innate mental ability and education are, of course, the most important factors in being "analytical"; but there are things you can do to increase your potential in this area:

- Think through a problem situation before you suggest a solution; then test your solution on several colleagues. Incorporate their feedback if warranted. (Remember, you can also ignore their feedback if you do not think it makes sense to incorporate it.)
- Gather as much background material as you can before tackling an issue, and learn from your own and others' previous successes and failures.

- Remain flexible. Never become so wedded to a solution that you can't alter or amend it (or even discard it) in the face of new evidence.

People who are expected to do (or to analyze) research, either primary or secondary, in connection with their jobs need analytical skills to sift through material, establish priorities, and sort the essential from the nonessential.

LANGUAGE SKILLS

"Language skills," or the ability to write clearly and to present one's ideas in an articulate manner when speaking, are essential to success in most jobs, though many studies have shown that speaking in front of a group is a cause of great anxiety in many people. The more professionally you can present yourself, the more seriously you will be taken, and the more effective you will be in doing your job.

In addition to being an asset in most jobs, advanced language skills form the specific basis of corporate communications and marketing communications activities at corporations and consulting firms. Communications departments have need of editors, writers, presentation consultants, and clear thinkers who can organize and present their own ideas and can help other people present their ideas clearly.

While it is not the purpose of this book to help you develop language skills—volumes exist on how to write and how to give a speech—the following few tips will help you make the best of the communications skills you already have:

- Think before you write or speak. Whether your medium is a memo or a 40-page report, or whether your forum is a telephone or an auditorium, know your subject well and determine what points you wish to make before you take pen to paper or open your mouth.
- Organize your words with a purpose in mind. Know what it is you want your audience to think or do, and structure your argument to achieve this goal.

- Deliver verbal messages and presentations with confidence. When speaking, stand straight and still and
  look people in the eye. (If you have a large audience,
  let your gaze meet the eyes of several people in the
  audience.) Speak clearly, slowly, and forcefully
  enough to be heard and understood, and dramatically
  enough to maintain the attention of your audience.
- Illustrate your points with vivid, concrete examples.
  Provide case histories when appropriate. People remember a story that proves a point long after they can
  recall an unillustrated statement.
- Whenever possible, seek feedback on your writing or
  your oral presentations. We can all use improvement,
  even when we are at the height of our powers.

If you are conversant in a foreign language, you possess an
additional marketable skill. Many businesses these days—-par-
ticularly large corporations—are multinational in scope and activity, and have a need for people who can deal with foreign
clients and customers in their own languages, or who can trans-
late and interpret written material. Languages such as Spanish,
German, and French are in great demand in the business world,
as are Japanese, Chinese, and Korean; but even languages that
fewer Americans are famliar with, such as Portuguese or Rus-
sian, are often very marketable to companies whose business
involves parts of the world where these languages are spoken.

"Language skills" also include the language of business. Develop a knowledge of your own industry's terminology—and of
the concepts and products underlying the terminology. It is impossible to succeed in a staff job, or any other job, if you don't
know what the business is about, and worse, if you don't seem
to care. Learn to speak knowledgeably about the business, and
to project your enthusiasm for it. Read, listen, talk to people to
gain this knowledge.

QUANTITATIVE AND TECHNICAL SKILLS

The more technical and mathematical knowledge and ability
you have, the more "quantitative" you are. Many jobs require
number-crunching abilities and/or some kind of technical exper-

tise. (Though many others, of course, do not.) Such skills, even if limited, are often very useful, as they place you in a pool of applicants smaller than the general group. Extensive skills of this sort are often highly rewarded, and in some cases can even compensate for the lack of other skills in a candidate.

Quantitative and technical skills are acquired through a disciplined educational process, either formal (at school) or informal (independently). Knowledge in math, statistics, and computer science, among other subjects, is very much in demand in the business world these days, in both line and support departments.

MANAGERIAL SKILLS

Every professional in the business world "manages": some manage people; others manage projects; and some manage both people and projects. Some skills that managers need are interpersonal—dealing fairly and firmly with subordinates; and some are analytical—problem-solving abilities. But some are skills that fit into neither the interpersonal nor the analytical category, yet are essential to managers. These include:

- *Setting priorities*   Most jobs today are too filled with duties, details, tasks, and obligations for employees trying to do these jobs to complete everything perfectly, even if they work late hours and take home attache cases filled with material each night. Knowing how to recognize what is most important for your department and your firm is a must in setting up a pecking order for your work and for the work of your subordinates. Learn how to decide what is most important, and to allocate the largest share of time and energy to the most important work—that which will most effectively accomplish your company's strategies and goals. Determine which projects require less attention, and learn to say "no" if the work should not be among your priorities.
- *Organizing*   Plan your hours, days, and weeks; break up projects into logical task sequences, and assign

each task to a person (or, if you are doing the project yourself, to a time slot). Organize the time of the people who report to you so that they fulfill the tasks for which your department is responsible. Discipline yourself to follow the organization plans you have established; and meet your own deadlines. Write out your plans, step by step, so you know what you have to do, and when. Minimize interruptions by having your phone calls screened and then returning them all at once and by encouraging people to make appointments with you and not just drop into your office except in emergencies. And be sure you allow yourself enough time to relax and unwind. Stress does not contribute to efficiency.

- *Tracking* Keep track of your projects and those of your subordinates by establishing a logical system and writing it out (on paper, on charts, on a computer screen). Follow up on all of your projects frequently, and leave yourself reminders on your calendar if the deadlines for certain tasks are some time away. An efficient manager doesn't ignore details.

- *Delegating* The more people and projects you manage, the more important it is to learn to delegate tasks and responsibilities. You will not always be able to do everything yourself; and at any rate, doing so will not help you develop a responsible staff. First, get to know your staff—what you can trust them to do well and what you can't. Then assign them tasks and responsibilities in an increasing manner. Monitor their progress frequently, but do not take over their responsibilities unless they have clearly failed. And do not forget to praise your subordinates when they perform well.

Managerial skills can be developed and are often the result of experience. You can enhance your managerial skills through courses and seminars, by reading the appropriate literature, by observing successful (and unsuccessful) managers, and, perhaps most important of all, by learning from your own mistakes.

TEACHING SKILLS

The ability to convey your knowledge to others is not confined to the classroom. Teaching goes on all the time—when you train new subordinates, when you educate sales and marketing people about a new product, when you deal with customers and clients, and when you explain a new system you have developed. Most jobs require some degree of teaching ability. Moreover, some people are hired by corporations to do nothing but teach, or develop training programs. Training jobs— usually part of the human resources function, but also occasionally found in line areas— are very much within your reach if you have a background in education, even if you are not an industry specialist in any business area. And so are speech coaching jobs.

If you can explain things clearly, encourage and inspire others, prepare logical educational plans, and be innovative and responsive in your approach to conveying information, you can make good use of these skills in the business world—not just in staff areas, but in line jobs as well.

The professional direction you choose to pursue should be determined by the skills and interests you have. As Peters and Waterman say in *In Search of Excellence,* it is important to find "a particular niche where you are better at something than anybody else."[1]

In considering the vast array of staff jobs, think about how your strengths and needs match the requirements of certain career paths. In the chart below, the types of jobs listed in chapter 2 of this book are categorized in terms of which job skills are most necessary for which jobs.

While in reality every job entails a bit of every skill listed, those skills marked with an "x" are of particular relevance to

[1]Thomas J. Peters and Robert H. Waterman, Jr., *In Search of Excellence* (New York: Harper & Row, 1982), p. 182.

Skill \ Function	Security management	Food service managment	Facilities management	Purchasing	Information management	Corporate giving	Corporate events	Community relations	Manpower planning	Professional recruitment	Clerical recruitment	Development/training	Benefits/compensation	Staff relations
Managerial	×	×	×	×	×		×	×	×	×				×
Teaching												×		×
Technical (knowledge of business or function)		×	×		×				×	×		×		
Language (written)						×						×	×	
Language (oral)							×	×	×	×	×			×
Analytical (problem solving)	×			×					×			×	×	
Interpersonal	×		×			×	×	×	×	×	×	×		×

Function

Administrative

Community affairs

Human resources

Skill \ Function	Communications	Public relations	Investor relations	Issues analysis	Speech writing	Presentation coaching	Publications work	A/V services	Advertising	Graphic design	Individual support jobs	Line planning support jobs
Managerial							×	×	×	×	×	
Teaching						×						
Technical (knowledge of business or function)	×	×	×	×			×	×	×	×		×
Language (written)	×	×	×	×			×		×	×	×	
Language (oral)	×				×	×		×				
Analytical (problem solving)	×	×	×	×	×	×			×	×	×	×
Interpersonal	×	×			×	×					×	

FIGURE 4–1 The Most Necessary Skills

the specific job indicated on the chart. Thus, administrative jobs (security management, food services, facilities, purchasing, or information) all require management skills; but security and facilities managers come into more contact with other people in their jobs than do information managers or food services directors and thus need greater interpersonal skills; those handling facilities and information need a more complex array of specific technical knowledge than security and purchasing managers do; and writing and language skills, while always useful, are less important than other skills for most administrative jobs.

Community affairs professionals, on the other hand, have a lot of interaction with many different types of people—community and professional groups, and both high- and low-level corporate employees—and have to be adept at dealing with all of them. And while these professionals need managerial skills and should be articulate, the level of specific technical knowledge they need does not have to be as high as it does for certain other functions.

If you are highly competent in interpersonal skills and also very articulate, you should probably consider personnel functions carefully in deciding on a career choice. You should consider communications if your analytical and writing skills are strong and if you know a lot about the company or field in which you want to work, (or if you are a quick learner). Notice from the chart that even within departments, different functions require different skills. Audio/video (A/V) professionals, for example, do not deal as much with other people as public relations professionals; but their technical knowledge about their work is extremely developed, while public relations professionals are more typically generalists. Individual support-staff jobs and line planning jobs primarily require strong managerial skills and good problem-solving abilities.

Matching your skills and interests to specific fields and jobs takes a good deal of time and much careful thought, but doing so is well worth the effort involved; being mismatched with a job can be a disaster. If you aim for a professional-level job with a future and that job is well-suited to you, your chances of success and happiness in that position are fairly high.

MIDCAREER HIRES

Most of the above considerations apply as well even if you are switching careers. Like some of their line counterparts, many staff employees have arrived on their present career paths because they were dissatisfied with another field or occupation. John Naisbitt explains the need for reshaping objectives this way: "when the situation changes, we must: (1) reconceptualize what business we are in, or (2) conceptualize what business it would be useful for us to think we are in. Furthermore, when the situation is constantly changing—as it is in today's world—the process of reconceptualization must itself be a constant process."[2]

The difference between entering a field right after college or professional school and entering later in the course of a career change is that though you are still at "entry level" when you switch careers, you will probably learn faster and get ahead sooner than your younger colleagues. The reason, of course, is that many skills—particularly analytical and interpersonal skills—are transferrable and universally necessary, and yours are likely to be more finely honed because you have used them in other arenas.

The key to making a career switch work is to figure out how to make your real experience count in your new field. Elizabeth Golden, for example, switched from academics to corporate communications in her late thirties. Although her teaching career had little to do with her new field at first glance, she did have some experience in managing projects, editing, writing, and negotiating. When interviewing for corporate communications jobs, she stressed every imaginable connection her past work had with her present intended track, and implied that her present goals represented not a real switch, but a logical extension of her previous work.

This illustration is not cited to imply that it is easy to make a career switch, but that working out a plausible strategy helps. Many employers in the business world are suspicious of career switchers, and look with disdain at any graduate or professional

[2]Naisbitt, pp. 93–4.

degree other than an MBA. Other employers, however, feel that employees with a nonstandard background often bring freshness and enthusiasm to their jobs and look at things in a new and perceptive way. When contemplating a career switch, consider it water under the bridge if you run into prospective employers such as the former, and try not to be discouraged. Even if you have had several rejections, you have to believe you will eventually find a job. In fact, if you give up and just go through the motions of looking for a position without believing you are worthy of a job, you are unlikely to land one.

For example, Bonnie Hillman had been a history teacher for eight years and then decided to shift her field. She went through a program for career changers given by one of the major graduate schools of business. When she completed the program and began applying for jobs, she faced a host of defamers of career switchers. The first interviewer thought she was over-qualified; the second thought she'd never come down from her "ivory tower"; the third insisted she was too old to learn; the fourth thought she'd demand too large a salary.

Bonnie's problem was that while *she* knew she had the right skills for human resources work, her professional experience did not demonstrate it directly. She had no business experience. She had to sell herself as an entry-level candidate with "potential," but most firms felt more comfortable with younger entry-level personnel who might not be "set in their ways" and might not demand as much in the way of salary and perks.

Finally, Bonnie met an interviewer whose background was similar to her own. The interviewer, a recruiter for a major insurance firm, not only found Bonnie charming and intelligent, but remembered how difficult it was to break into the field herself. She gave Bonnie all the start she needed by introducing her to someone in her corporation who was looking for a candidate with exceptional interpersonal skills, someone, the recruiter knew, who would look favorably on Bonnie's past academic experience.

Finding someone whose past resembles yours, however, is not always the way around a maverick background. Rebecca Hennesy, for example, managed an internal communications area in a large conglomerate. Although she had taught in a university before entering communications, she really did not believe that anyone else could make the transition as smoothly as she did, and consistently refused to look at any resumes other than ones representing a total, lifelong commitment to communications.

At times, the fault in not finding the right match lies with the applicant. Naomi Werther, for instance, applied for and was rejected by fifteen different companies when she entered the job market after taking the same crash program as Bonnie. Naomi continued sending out letters, but they began to sound more and more defeatist in tone, and prospective employers immediately picked this up. Naomi's fifteen rejections soon expanded to thirty, then to fifty before she stopped applying altogether. There were some concrete reasons for Naomi's lack of success. She hadn't defined her career goals; she hadn't bothered to research the industry in which she was job-seeking; and she made constant references to teaching and students when she should have been discussing the business work with interviewers. She should have done some reassessment before giving up, but she caved in to defeat and took herself out of the job market instead, firmly convinced that the program she had taken was a failure.

If you are considering a career switch, be sure to ask yourself why you were unhappy or unproductive in your former occupation. Look for the underlying reason—was it the environment? the nature of the work? the skills required? the pay? your fellow workers? the opportunities for growth?—and try to select a new area where these problems do not recur. Too many people switch careers only to find that they misjudged the situation and re-created the problems they thought they were leaving behind.

Don't be overhasty in abandoning a line of work. At times, a change of locale is enough to infuse fresh life into a career. A sizable percentage of career switchers either feel they made a mistake in changing and have to live with it, or switch back to their first type of position after realizing that they were really dissatisfied with the superficial, not the intrinsic, aspects of their first jobs.

The take-home lesson here, whether you are entering a new field at the beginning of your career or making a career switch, is to structure your self-assessment in such a way as to match your needs and skills to the opportunities available in various fields. It isn't easy, but it's well worth the effort to analyze yourself and to learn about the business world in some depth before entering the job marketplace.

Chapter 5
Getting Hired

Once you have figured out your own strengths and weaknesses, as well as what job or field meets your needs, the next step is to begin the job search. While there are probably as many ways of getting a job as there are jobs, there are some generalities that can be made about a job search. For example, in most fields, the best way of finding a job is through personal contacts, or "networking." This does not mean that you have to have an uncle or a sister-in-law in the field in which you wish to secure a job, but that if you have any friends, relatives, or friends-of-friends in a given area, you should call them to ask about job openings.

As we mentioned in the last chapter, don't be afraid to contact people you know, or people mentioned to you by friends. Ask them about their jobs—what they do, how they like it, what kinds of people their companies hire, what their backgrounds were like. If you are seeking information about certain kinds of professions, you will be surprised at how helpful some people are, even if they do not know you. While some people you approach might not welcome your intrusion, others will remember the beginning of their career and will be more understanding.

If you are already in a field, or if you are absolutely sure you want to enter it, you can ask directly about whether there are any opportunities for employment; if you are not certain about whether you would fit in a certain mode of employment, or you have no direct experience in a given area, your best bet is to ask whether your contact can see you for an informational interview. As we explained in chapter 4, asking an employee about what he or she does and about the field in general is not putting that person on the spot, as it is when you ask whether any jobs are available. People will often be more receptive to someone calling for information than for someone looking for a job. In fact, even if you know you want a certain kind of job, calling a contact for "information" is often an easier way of getting in to see someone than asking about job availability; and once you are in the door, unexpected opportunities may arise. It is always possible that one of the people you contact might be looking for someone with just your qualifications.

For example, Karen Oserly thought corporate communications was an interesting area, especially for an ex-journalist. She had a friend whose fiancé was in PR at a major accounting firm in New York, and Karen gave him a call. He asked her to the firm for lunch and for a couple of hours they discussed the kinds of work writers could do in corporations. At the end of lunch the PR man, who was impressed with Karen's intelligence, called the head of publications, who he knew was on the lookout for a writer, and she called Karen in for an interview. Karen never once asked her contact for a job, or if he knew of any openings in his firm, but she made it clear she was interested in this kind of work. Though she didn't get the job for which she was interviewed because her experience wasn't extensive enough, the head of publications was also impressed with Karen and a month later, when a junior writer on her staff quit unexpectedly, she offered Karen that job.

If you have contacts in a given field and they seem interested in your career search, call them back from time to time. Most people, if they think your skills are good enough, won't be adverse to mentioning your name when an opening comes up. You don't want to call so often you become a pest, but a call every now and then shouldn't be taken amiss. One employee at a major commercial bank will freely give job information to those contacting him, but never calls them when he knows of a job. He doesn't feel he wants to act the part of a headhunter, and he believes anyone who really wants a position will be a bit aggressive. If an employee does agree to see you, whether for "information" or for a possible job opening, don't abuse his or her kindness. Have your questions ready and don't hang around for hours. And limit your inquiries to business. One young woman who agreed to meet a recent graduate of her MBA school for an "information" interview was flabbergasted when at the end of the interview he asked her whether she knew any single women in the area. She was so annoyed she threw away his resume, even though there was an opening in her department for which he might have qualified. And another young man, who had spoken with several kindhearted classmates in various fields when he was looking for a job, annoyed them all when he appeared unannounced at their offices a few weeks later, trying to sell them insurance. A few of these people felt betrayed enough to refuse to see other candidates "networking" from their business school.

Other ways of finding job opportunities are: if you are at school, through on-campus interviews; through professional organizations (both personal contacts and published job lists); through newspaper and journal advertisements, and through reputable headhunters.

Looking for a job can be frustrating, but you should not get discouraged. If you answer an ad—in a journal, newspaper, or job list—remember that you are probably one of dozens or even hundreds responding to the same ad, and that while some ad respondents actually land the jobs for which they have applied, most do not even receive an acknowledgement of their letters. Headhunters, too, can be frustrating to deal with. Be sure that in selecting a headhunter, you contact one whose specialities include the fields in which you are interested and who places people at your level. And be sure to select only those headhunters whose fees are paid by corporations, not by the individual job-seekers. It is best to choose a headhunter on the recommendation of someone in the field in which you are interested, or from a list of those advertising in a specialized professional journal. If you are not sure who pays the fee, inquire. Headhunters who are paid by companies to recruit for various positions usually have real jobs to fill, whereas those whom the candidate pays often do not. If you are successful in a field, you will probably have a list of headhunters of your own because they will contact you, even if you are not officially in the job market.

When you begin your job search, go to places in a hiring mode. Read the newspapers and look at economic magazines and reports and try to assess which industries are growing and therefore hiring. Focus your search on them. Base your assessment not only on what is happening in the economy at the present time, but on what, in your best estimate, is likely to happen in the near future.

Growing industries are likely to be fruitful hunting grounds for job opportunities. But make sure they are not glutted industries. The biotechnology industry and the microcomputer industry are cases in point. Extreme public interest in both recently spawned dozens of new companies in these areas, and these companies hired hundreds of new employees. Many of the companies created by the technological revolutions in both fields are producing products and have not only survived, but are growing; other companies folded as quickly as they were set up, taking their employees down with them.

Be smart about switching from one industry to another. If you have been squeezed out of one industry—the publishing industry comes to mind as being a difficult industry to get a good job in nowadays—don't turn around and try to enter an equally difficult area. For example, if you can't make inroads into publishing, forget about related fields such as the telecommunications industry or the media.

It is important to consider general economic trends as well as specific growth areas in choosing a field. Is the economy going up or down? Is a recession going on? Is inflation out of hand? General economic conditions affect companies' hiring practices, and if you're looking for a job, you should be savvy about what is going on in the economy and be smart about where you look. No company or industry is recession-proof. For example, commercial banks feel recessions later than other companies and might be in a hiring mode longer than other companies; the flip side, however, is that banks feel recoveries later than other companies and might still be feeling the pinch when other companies have lifted their hiring freezes.

THE RESUME

When you are assessing your skills and preparing yourself for the job search, put together a solid business resume at the same time. Enclose this resume with all your inquiry letters, and bring several copies with you whenever you are speaking with someone in the business world—whether on a job interview or an informational interview, even when you are networking informally—so that person can keep a copy of your resume or pass it along to someone else.

In many instances the resume you send is the first impression you will make on a contact or prospective employer. Therefore, the resume has to help you put your best foot forward. To do this it has to be concise, concrete, and descriptive. Modesty might prevent you from being too forward about your accomplishments in a cover letter or even at a meeting or interview, while in a resume you can list your accomplishments objectively, projecting the image of yourself that you wish to convey.

Business resumes should be no more than one page long, and consequently should contain only information pertinent to the qualifications necessary for the jobs for which you are applying. They should be as sparsely written as possible.

All resumes should contain your full name and both your home and business address and telephone numbers at the top. Follow this by a section labeled "Objective," which states the specific kind of job you are seeking—and in which area or industry. To be this specific in a resume, you will need several different versions for the several different types of corporations or businesses to which you might be applying. It is important to include the "Objective" section in your resume so that you appear focused and so that the prospective employer is aware of this focus. Don't worry about being shut out of other kinds of jobs because you have been too specific in stating your objective. If an employer thinks your qualifications look right for another type of job, he will ask you about it even if you haven't indicated a direct interest on your resume. However, if your resume does not look centered on *any* area, you will be dismissed as being unfocused. Few employers are going to want to waste time on candidates whose resumes indicate they don't know their own strengths and don't know what they want to do.

After focusing your resume, be sure that everything that follows supports your indicated career objective. Emphasize those skills and experiences which demonstrate that you can do the kind of job you say you want.

Make the next category an overall "Personal Profile," in which you briefly state your professional strengths. Again, be sure these strengths are consistent with the requirements of the job you want. Then list your job experience in reverse chronological order, beginning with the most recent job; indicate for each job not only where and when you held it, but the types of functions and responsibilities it entailed.

If your past job experience is not exactly relevant to your present job objective, you should prepare what is known as a "functional" resume instead of a chronological one. Make the "Professional Experience" category "Functional Experience" instead. Here, list the functions you performed in jobs you have held, then list your jobs briefly in reverse chronological order. If you have no job experience, list the functions you know you can perform and tell where you have performed these functions in the past—in courses, extracurricular or community activities, etc.

The next category is "Education": list degrees and academic majors, especially those relevant to your job objective. Include major educational programs you have attended or professional certificates you have earned, and for all provide dates and institutions and their locations. Do not include a course list or grades. Few business employers care about this. If for some reason they do, they can ask you for additional information or talk to you about it at the interview. If you have earned any major honors—elected membership in professional societies or special academic awards such as Phi Beta Kappa, for example—you can include an "Honors" category. There is a good reason for including this information: it shows you are capable of exceptional performance; but keep this section brief.

Similarly, briefly include any special information you feel will help make you stand out, such as publications or foreign language fluency. You do not have to include any personal information (marital status, whether you have children, age, health, etc.). The law does not allow prospective employers to ask for this type of information. Don't include information about hobbies; doing so appears frivolous. If you believe information regarding personal matters or hobbies would help your case, bring it up at the interview. Also, do not list references in a resume. If prospective employers want them further on down the road, they will ask. If you are looking at jobs outside your geographical area, indicate on the resume that you are willing to relocate.

Remember that these resume categories are not carved in stone. They are only examples of possible categories. Other categories might be more appropriate to your resume. In any case, adhere to the basic principles of resume writing: have focus, clearly describe your qualifications, be brief, and stick to one page. To keep your resume from becoming too wordy, use phrases instead of complete sentences.

The physical appearance of your resume is important, too. If you can, type it on a word processor and print it out on a letter-quality printer (using roman print, not italic). Be sure the spacing is consistent and, if possible, print the category heads in boldface. The general impression should be neat, organized, and pleasing to the eye. If you have to type the resume on the typewriter, use an electric one, use a carbon ribbon or a fresh cloth one, and make sure the machine's letters are well-aligned. Reproduce the resume on quality paper (white or offwhite heavy bond), and use a copying machine that doesn't leave shadows.

Two sample resumes, one functional and one chronological, are shown:

FUNCTIONAL RESUME

ADRIENNE O'CONNOR

Home Address:
423 West Haven Street
New Castle, Mass. 00011
Phone: 617-593-4321

Business Address:
Brook Bank, Inc.
101 East State Street
Windsor, Mass. 11111
Phone: 617-234-5678

CAREER OBJECTIVE:
Position as press writer in public relations department of large commercial bank.

PERSONAL PROFILE:
Highly developed research, writing, and editing skills; works well under pressure of deadlines; excellent interpersonal skills; some managerial experience.

PROFESSIONAL EXPERIENCE:
Research—Provided background research for in-depth economics journal articles written by Nebraska College Journalism Department Chairman.
Editing—Copyedited financial articles on town newspaper.
Writing—Wrote extensively in journalism school, gaining experience in economics and political writing in particular.
Interacting with press—Made many press contacts through Nebraska College Journalism School student press conferences; served on University seminar panels with reporters from several large city dailies.
Managing—Supervised junior writers while research assistant.

JOB HISTORY:
1983–85 Brook Bank, Windsor, Mass., Public Relations Department. Administrative Assistant.
1980–83 *The Baychester Chronicle,* Baychester, Mass. Copy editor.
1978–80 Journalism Department, Nebraska College, Lincoln, Nebraska. Research assistant to chairman.

EDUCATION:
B.A. Nebraska College, Lincoln, Nebraska, 1978 (Economics)
M.A. Nebraska College, Lincoln, Nebraska, 1980 (Journalism)

SPECIAL SKILLS:
Read and speak fluent French.

PUBLICATION:
Article on banking legislation developments for *The Baychester Chronicle,* Baychester Mass., April 19, 1979.

CHRONOLOGICAL RESUME

ADRIENNE O'CONNOR

Home Address:
423 West Haven Street
New Castle, Mass. 00011
Phone: 617-593-4321

Business Address:
Brook Bank, Inc.
101 East State Street
Windsor, Mass. 11111
Phone: 617-234-5678

CAREER OBJECTIVE:
  Position as press writer in public relations department of
  large commercial bank.

PERSONAL PROFILE:
  Highly developed research, writing, and editing skills; works
  well under pressure of deadlines; excellent interpersonal
  skills; some managerial experience.

PROFESSIONAL EXPERIENCE:
  1983–85   Brook Bank, Windsor, Mass., Public Relations
            Department. Administrative Assistant—handled
            details of press conferences; assisted writers with
            checking of facts; did some copyediting.
  1980–83   *The Baychester Chronicle* (circulation: 2,000),
            Baychester, Mass. Copy editor—copy-edited finan-
            cial articles; did some writing.
  1978–80   Journalism Department, Nebraska College,
            Lincoln, Nebraska. Research assistant to Chair-
            man—provided background research for in-depth
            economics journal articles written by Chairman;
            supervised junior writers; made many press con-
            tacts through student press conferences; served
            on University seminar panels with reporters from
            several large city dailies; wrote extensively, gain-
            ing experience in economics and political writing
            in particular.

EDUCATION:
  B.A.   Nebraska College, Lincoln, Nebraska, 1978
            (Economics)

M.A.   Nebraska College, Lincoln, Nebraska, 1980
(Journalism)

SPECIAL SKILLS:
Read and speak fluent French.

PUBLICATION:
Article on banking legislation developments for *The Baychester Chronicle,* Baychester Mass., April 19, 1979.

THE COVER LETTER

Whether sending out your resume in response to an advertisement or applying to a company or executive-search firm for a position, pay particular attention to the cover letter you include. The cover letter, like the resume, is part of your first introduction to the employer or recruiter. How you present yourself in writing can determine whether your application will be a success or a failure. The letter should say enough to suggest that you are a viable applicant, and it should make the reader think it would be worth his or her time to peruse your resume. It is also the first indication a prospective employer has about whether you can communicate clearly, which is important for any job.

A cover letter should be short—one-half to three-fourths of a page—but should nonetheless contain some crucial information. Begin by stating precisely for what position or type of position you are applying, and if relevant, at whose suggestion you are writing. (It always helps to have an entree.) If you are answering an ad, state as much and say where you saw the ad. Be sure to state explicitly why you want the job, then immediately zero in on a few of the qualifications you have that make you a viable candidate for the job. You must get to the point immediately, because you have to assume the reader

- May be busy.
- May be the recipient of many such applications.

- May not be enthused about receiving unsolicited applications.

You want the reader to focus on your letter whether he or she is inclined to do so or not; make it direct, succinct, and professional.

Support your claim to having certain skills necessary for the job by stating briefly the relevant experience in which you have demonstrated these skills. You also might use your cover letter to highlight a relevant quality or experience that your resume does not stress, which might be overlooked in a quick reading of your resume.

Close your letter by saying that you are attaching a copy of your resume, and that you hope to hear from the employer in the near future. Even better, state that you will call him or her in a few days to try to arrange an interview. State also that references and, if relevant, work samples are available on request. Don't forget to thank the person for his or her attention. Remember to check your grammar and spelling, and to be sure the letter is neat and professional looking.

A sample cover letter, answering an ad for a corporate communications position, follows:

Dear _____:

In response to the ad placed in the May 1, 1985, Boston *Globe,* I would like to apply for the position of senior writer for an in-house publication in a major financial institution. I have a strong editing and writing background, and I also have some experience with editorial production.

I have worked for four years as a junior writer and production assistant for a corporate magazine at XYZ Corporation in Dallas, Texas. Although I have enjoyed the work at XYZ, and although I have learned a great deal about writing, reporting, and professional interactions in a corporation, I now feel my experience is sufficient to make a move to a more challenging position. I have always been interested in financial institutions (I was an economics major in college), and I would welcome the opportunity to relocate to Boston, where I grew up.

I am enclosing my resume with this letter. Writing samples and references are available on request. I will be in Boston for two weeks, beginning April 12, to visit my family. I will telephone you on Monday, April 14, to try to arrange an interview at your convenience to discuss my application further.

Thank you for your attention.

Sincerely,

There may be occasions when a longer, more detailed cover letter is appropriate. If you know a job exists, and you know many of its requirements, or if you have been invited to apply for a position, you might wish to go into more detail in presenting your qualifications for the position. In addition, if you know the position is in an organization where the work pace is not hurried and they are carefully considering only a few candidates, you might want to provide a longer cover letter. In any case, however, try not to exceed two pages. Few people want to wade through a seemingly endless letter, and your extra efforts will be self-defeating. Moreover, you want to save something to say at the interview.

THE INTERVIEW

After having sent out a resume and cover letter and landed an interview—whether a real job interview or an information interview—there is a lot you can do to make it a success. First, do your homework. Talk to people who know the area or the corporation. Go to the business library and read all you can (books, articles, annual reports, studies) about the field, industry, and company for which you will be interviewed, and then write out a series of questions you think an interviewer might logically ask. While one can never anticipate everything an interviewer might ask, there are many questions that are fairly standard at interviews and really don't change from job to job or field to field. For example,

- Why do you want to work in this industry? Or at this particular job?
- How do you think you can make a contribution to this organization?
- Why do you want to change jobs?
- What are your strengths?
- What are your weak points?
- Do you have any questions?

You had better have good answers to all of these questions if you expect an interviewer to take you seriously. Having researched the field, you should be able to say what interests you about it and what you think you can bring to it. The more you know about the specific job, the more you can tailor your own experiences to fit the needs of the position. If you know very little about the job, ask about it; if asking brings no information, try to imagine what it would entail and how your skills would fit in. The best of all possible situations is to know enough about the job and the line of work to make some actual suggestions regarding what the company is doing, but such a situation is rare except at fairly high professional levels. Be sure you exude enthusiasm about the position and the line of work. No one wants to hire a lackluster person who does not get turned on by the job for which he or she is applying. One unsuccessful candidate for an analyst's job in a trade department at a major financial institution jokingly termed some aspects of the job "boring." While they, indeed, probably were just that, the interviewer did not think the candidate's categorization was amusing and dismissed him on the spot.

In answering the question about why you want to change jobs, be as positive as possible. Stress enhanced career opportunity, a chance to learn new things, a change of direction, a place to practice newly acquired skills, rather than something negative about your past job. Above all, do not complain about your last boss. If you say negative things about your last position or employer, even if true, you will appear a whiner or, worse, a failure. Everyone knows that people don't change jobs unless they are dissatisfied about something; but a prospective employer is really not asking you to elaborate on these gripes. He or she really wants to learn something about your attitude: Were you a troublemaker? Were you a pest? If you were passed over for advancement or you were fired, why? And how did you react to the situation? Try to structure your answers so as to appear a positive employee and a contributing force in a department. Even if you were fired or passed over—and you obviously have to own up if this is the case because most prospective employers check candidates' work histories—don't seem bitter about your previous situation. Explain that conditions changed and you were unprepared for the new technology, or that you were never really a good match for the particular job, or that your real strengths were in a different area.

Most candidates have no trouble talking about their strengths. It is important to remember, however, that the strengths you mention must be related to the job for which you are applying. Being good with people, for example, is not relevant if you are applying for a library research job where you sit behind closed doors for hours at a time. Some candidates are shy and think modesty has a place in the interview process. Don't be obnoxious about yourself, but do mention your skills and accomplishments in a nice way, and point out how they will fit in the employer's organization. Use the opportunity provided by this type of question to tell prospective employers what you want them to know about you and your experience. Come with your own agenda in this regard.

Many candidates have more trouble with the almost invariable question about weaknesses. While it would be illuminating for a would-be boss to learn that, try as you might, you can never make it in by nine, he or she is not really likely to hire you if you mention this as a weakness; and he or she will think you a fool for mentioning it. The hirer does not, moreover, really want to hear that you have no weaknesses. While you may not want to mention real drawbacks, which you are hoping to improve on anyway, you have to say something, or the interviewer will simply believe you have not really prepared for the interview. What you can do is to give as a negative something that will really stand you in good stead: "I really am a bit of a workaholic." "I tend to be a perfectionist and keep at a project for extra weekends if need be to make it right." "I find it hard not to think about the office when I'm sailing." Don't overdo it, but come up with something "negative" that is really positive. In fact, if the employer does see workaholism, for example, as a negative, he or she will think you are making strides towards curing this ill by recognizing it.

Above all, don't ignore the invariable, "Are there any questions you might have?" Too many candidates whose interviews have gone well up to this point blow it because they do not ask any intelligent questions. The interviewer thinks such candidates are either uninterested in or uninformed about the position they are seeking. Prepare a list of meaty questions in advance about the kind of work the company does, the markets they focus on, the size of their business, the type of people who work there, the candidate qualifications being sought, the day-to-day activities involved. Memorize these questions!

The first interview, by the way, is not the place for questions about salary, vacation time, or benefits. If you don't already know, you can discuss ranges to make sure that you and the employer are in the same ball park, but hold the nitty-gritty questions for later. You want to appear eager to do the type of work involved, challenging work you can grow with. You do not want to appear simply interested in material rewards. And by all means, save any special requests (extended time off, unusual medical needs) for later—after they have made the offer and really want you.

The second thing you can do to ensure that an interview goes as well as possible is to practice. Have a friend or relative ask you the questions you have anticipated, and make believe you are really at the interview. Talk out the answers, don't just think them out. Let the friend or relative criticize your answers—and your deportment. If you can videotape the interview, all the better. You'll soon notice exactly where you need improvement. If you can neither videotape your practice interview, nor get together with another person, ask and answer your own questions in front of a mirror. Practice standing tall, shaking hands firmly, looking people in the eye frequently without staring, smiling when appropriate, and looking controlled, yet relaxed. Dress appropriately for the company you are visiting. The prototypical blue interview suit is often correct, but not always. It is best to figure out what kind of clothes and accessories are acceptable in your chosen line of work and invest in something suitable. (The new garment won't go to waste; you'll be able to wear it out after you get the job.)

One more piece of advice: leave the interview on a positive note. Ask what the next steps will be and then thank the interviewer and tell him or her you're interested in the job. It may sound corny, but he or she really wants to know this. Then follow up immediately with a typed, accurately addressed thank-you note, stressing again how informative and interesting the interview was. If possible, include some words—or article or clipping—relevant to some point you discussed at the interview, just to emphasize how taken you are with the subject. Follow the note with a call a few weeks later if you haven't heard from the interviewer. He or she really might not be interested, but on the other hand, a reminder of the fact that you are interested might just keep you in the running. Be polite and follow the forms even if the interview didn't go well. You never know who's talking to whom in the business world.

Lila Stair, in *Careers in Business,* offers some additional concrete advice about going on an interview:

> Set yourself up for a successful interview by making sure that your first impression on the interviewer is a good one because it will be a lasting one. Neat, conservative dress is recommended. Women should wear a simply tailored suit, a neat hairdo, only plain jewelry, and moderate makeup and perfume. Men should wear a conservative suit, shirt, and tie. Polished shoes, trimmed and styled hair, and clean fingernails contribute to a man's overall appearance.
>
> Be early rather than late. If you are late, the interviewer will have less time to spend with you and you will be unable to make as many points in your favor. Also, if you arrive late, your reliability might be questioned.
>
> Attempt to project a courteous and enthusiastic image. You should be looking forward to the interview as an opportunity to promote yourself and to gain information about the company and the position available. If you have prepared yourself and are confident in your appearance, you will be

calm, not nervous, and able to look upon the interview for the opportunity that it is.

Although each interview will be unique, there are usually four phases in an interview. The first phase is devoted to breaking the ice and establishing a climate for the exchange of information. It may involve humor, small talk, and a few simple questions that clarify items on your resume.

The second phase of the interview is the hard part. During this phase the interviewer will attempt to get as much information from you as possible. Always remember that the interviewer controls the interview. Be patient and answer all questions carefully. You will have an opportunity to ask the questions before the interview is complete. Your responses to the interviewer's questions demonstrate your performance under pressure, quickness, effectiveness, energy, sense of humor, and grammar. Expect some broad questions such as "How would you describe yourself as a person?" and "How can you contribute to our organization?" Remember that the interviewer is looking at both substance, which is basically your past performance, and style, which includes communication skills, poise, self-confidence, and motivation. Broad questions reveal how you organize your thoughts, your values, your personality, and even how you might be to work with.

No matter how mentally exhausted you are after answering the interviewer's questions, summon up some energy for the third phase of the interview, because it's your turn to ask the questions. The interviewer will probably ask if you have any questions. You always should! Such topics as training possibilities and other opportunities for professional growth, advancement possibilities, the average age of persons in the next level up in the company, and how many people were hired in the last few recruiting seasons are all things you might like to know. Focus on *opportunities* for your professional growth and work-related activities. Wait until the job is offered to you, then ask questions about such things as vacations and retirement.

The final phase may be summary of what has been said, an indication of when you should expect to hear from the company, and friendly words of departure. You should remember to thank the interviewer. The interest in you shown by the interviewer does not mean that you will get the job. It

> is standard operating procedure; the interviewer is building goodwill and *keeping you interested.* Don't cancel your other interviews. Even if you have a firm job offer, compare it against what other companies have to offer when you are just beginning your career.[1]

Professional recruiters are trained to look for certain things when interviewing candidates, and keeping these in mind might help you in preparing for your interview. According to information prepared for interviewers by the Drake Beam Morin, Inc., consulting firm, employment interviewers are trying to determine whether a candidate *can* do a certain job, whether he or she *will* do the job if hired, and how that person will *fit* into the organization. In trying to determine these things, interviewers assess the candidate's communication skills, intellectual abilities, leadership potential, and personality (their enthusiasm, maturity, and integrity).

According to consultants Henry H. Morgan, Michael H. Frisch, and John W. Cogger, of the above firm, an interviewer should structure an interview in these categories:

    I. Introduction
   II. Work Experience
  III. Education
  IV. Present Activities & Interest
   V. Summary of Strengths
  VI. Summary of Shortcomings
 VII. Closing Remarks[2]

The following* are questions these consultants recommend that interviewers ask candidates:

GREETING
(Spontaneous)

[1]Lila B. Stair, *Careers in Business* (Homewood, Illinois: Richard D. Irwin, Inc., 1980), pp. 181–2.

[2]Henry H. Morgan, Michael H. Frisch, and John W. Cogger, *Seven Imperatives!* (Drake Beam Morin, Inc., 1980), pp. 181–2.

*From *Seven Imperatives!* by Henry H. Morgan, Michael H. Frisch & John W. Cogger, Copyright © 1980 by Drake Beam Morin, Inc. Reprinted by permission of the publisher.

SMALL TALK
(Improvise)

OPENING QUESTION (Select one or more)
How did you happen to become interested in our organization?
What is your understanding of the job for which you are applying?
What has been your contact with our organization?

INTRODUCTION
Today, I'd like to talk with you about your background and experience. If we get to know you well—what you've done—and what you hope to do—then we can judge whether we have opportunities in our organization that are suited to your talents and interests. Certainly, it's to your advantage as well as ours to become well acquainted with each other before making an employment decision.

So—I'd like to hear about your jobs, schooling, interests and hobbies, and anything else that you would like to tell me. Perhaps a good place to start is with your work experience (continue below):

WORK EXPERIENCE
Tell me about the jobs you've held, what your duties and responsibilities were, and what you liked or didn't like about the jobs. Also, I'm interested in your level of earnings, any special achievements you may have had, and what you think you gained from these jobs.

Let's begin with your earliest jobs—those you may have had after school and during the summers. What do you remember about your very first job?

EDUCATION
You've given me a good picture of your work experience. Now let's talk about your education. I'd like to know a little about your early schooling—and then, of course, more about recent schooling, including any specialized training you've had. I'd be interested in such things as—the subjects you preferred, those you didn't like so much, your grades, extracurricular activities, and any special recognition you received. What was your earliest schooling like?

PRESENT ACTIVITIES AND INTERESTS (Optional)
We've talked about your work and schooling. Now, let's talk about your leisure time activities—your interests or hobbies. What do you like to do for fun and recreation—either on your own, or with others?

SUMMARY OF STRENGTHS (Assets)

Now, let's try to summarize our conversation. Thinking about what we've covered today, what would you say are some of your chief strengths? This is your chance to brag a little! What are some of the assets that would make you a good prospect for any employer?

SUMMARY OF SHORTCOMINGS (Development needs)

You've given me some real strengths—but what about some of your abilities or qualities that aren't so strong? All of us have a few areas we wish to develop further. In the past, you may have had constructive criticism from friends, supervisors, or others who knew you well. Thinking of the future, what areas or what personal qualities need improvement for you to be fully effective in your job or career?

CLOSING REMARKS

You've given me a good review of your background and experience! I've enjoyed talking with you, and I appreciate your sharing this information with me—it will be of value to us in making our decision. Before we close, what else would you like to cover? What questions would you like to ask me about the job, our organization, or anything else? (Dialogue; answer questions; give information; sell, if appropriate).

CORDIAL PARTING
(Spontaneous)

The way an interview goes should tell you something about how you are doing. The above consultants say: "if the interview process is working well, then the chances are very good that the content of the interview will be rich and useful. If the process is not working well, then the content of the interview is likely to be spoiled."[3]

If, despite all your preparation, the interview is a total disaster, chalk it up to experience and learn from your mistakes. Chances are you won't make the same errors again, and if the interview really went poorly, you probably weren't a good match for the position anyway. It's better to learn you don't fit at an interview than after you accept the job.

[3]Ibid.

Figure 5-1 illustrates what these consultants feel interviewers should look for in a candidate during the interview process.

TOPICS	LINE OF INQUIRY	JOB QUALIFICATIONS
Introduction		
Cover:		Look for:
Greeting		Appearance
Small talk		Manner
Opening question(s)		Self-expression
Lead question		Responsiveness
Work experience		
Cover:	Ask:	Look for:
Earliest jobs, part-time, temporary	Things done best?	Relevance of work
	Done less well?	Sufficiency of work
Military assignments	Things liked best?	Skill and competence
	Liked less well?	
Full-time positions	Major accomplishments? How achieved?	Adaptability
Volunteer work		Productivity
	Most difficult problems faced? How handled?	Motivation
		Interpersonal relations
	Ways most effective with people? Ways less effective?	Leadership
		Growth and development
	Level of earnings?	
	Reasons for changing jobs?	
	What learned from work experience?	
	What looking for in job? In career?	
	Short-term and long-range goals?	
Education		
Cover:	Ask:	Look for:
(Elementary school)	Best subjects? Subjects done less well?	Relevance of schooling
High school		
College	Subjects liked most?	Sufficiency of schooling
	Liked least?	
Specialized training	Reactions to teachers?	Intellectual abilities
Recent courses		Versatility

FIGURE 5-1 The Interview Process

TOPICS	LINE OF INQUIRY	JOB QUALIFICATIONS
Education Cover:	Ask: Level of grades? Effort required? Reasons for choos- ing school? Major field? Special achieve- ments? Toughest problems? Role in extracurricu- lar activities? How financed education? Relation of educa- tion to career? Consider further schooling or spe- cialized training?	Look for: Breadth and depth of knowledge Level of accom- plishment Motivation and interests Reaction to authority Leadership Teamwork
Present activities and **interests** (Optional) Cover: Special interests and hobbies Civic and commu- nity affairs that are job-relevant Health and energy Geographical preferences	Ask: Things like to do in spare time? Extent involved in community? What kind of health problems might affect job perfor- mance? Reaction to reloca- tion? to travel? Circumstances that might influence job performance?	Look for: Vitality Management of time, energy, money Maturity and judgment Intellectual growth Cultural breadth Diversity of interests Social effectiveness Interpersonal skills and interests Leadership Basic values and goals Situational factors
Summary of strengths **and shortcomings** Cover: Strengths (Assets)	Ask: What bring to job? What are assets?	Look for: PLUS (+) AND MINUS (−)

FIGURE 5-1 Continued

TOPICS	LINE OF INQUIRY	JOB QUALIFICATIONS
Summary of strengths and shortcomings		
Cover:	Ask:	Look for:
	What are best talents?	Can do?
		Talents, skills,
	What qualities seen by self or others?	Knowledge
		Energy
	What makes you a good investment for employer?	Will do?
		Motivation
		Interests
		How fit?
Cover:	Ask:	Personal qualities
Shortcomings	What are some	Social effective-
(Development	shortcomings or	ness
needs)	limitations?	Character
	What areas need	Situational factors
	improvement?	Synthesis
	What qualities wish	Zero prejudice
	to develop further?	(EEO)
	What constructive criticism from others?	
	How might you be a risk for employer?	
	What further training or experience might you need?	

From *Seven Imperatives!* by Henry H. Morgan, Michael H. Frisch & John W. Cogger; copyright © 1980 by Drake Beam Morin, Inc. Reprinted by permission of the publisher.

FIGURE 5-1 Concluded

There are, by the way, interviewers who delight in making people feel uncomfortable, and if a "stress" interviewer destroyed your meeting, learn from that, too. Stress interviewers are sometimes just mean, but often are purposely difficult to see how candidates react under extreme conditions. If the job for which you are applying demands concentration under trying circumstances, quick decisions, and a controlled reactive stance, the interviewer probably wants to see how you handle yourself under pressure. He or she might make outrageous statements about your lack of experience, interrupt you in the middle of an answer, question your sincerity about wanting to change jobs, or probe you on an area on which you are clearly underprepared. Your response in a case like this is to keep your cool, answer what you can, and then forget the whole ordeal. Don't let it shake you. You might come out just fine, and if you don't, you probably don't want to work with people like that anyway.

One young woman was convinced she wouldn't get a writing job because the interviewer told her her writing put his teeth on edge. Nonetheless she pressed him to be more specific, he pointed to several habitual idiosyncrasies in her writing, and she patiently explained that those forms were part of the culture of her last place of employ and that she had no objection to dropping those forms in another job. After several such sessions, she got the job—as much, she believes, for *how* she answered the stress questions as *what* she answered.

While stress interviews can have a place in the hiring process, if you find yourself in a stress interview that is getting too uncomfortable—for example, if the interviewer becomes too abusive, insinuating, racist or sexist—end the session and announce that you feel you would not be a good match for the job. Stress interviews have a logical end where human dignity begins.

LANDING THE JOB

Once the interview process is over—and it may take several long interviews and lunches and full-day meetings over a period of months—the rest is really largely up to you. If you are called back several times, the employer is extremely interested. You may be the only remaining candidate, or one of two or three, but you are definitely in the running. If asked for references at this point, think carefully. Give as references people who are lately familiar with your work, and who would be supportive of advancing your career. Avoid those with a grudge against you, those for whom you represent direct competition, a boss who doesn't want to lose you (or a boss who does), those whose own credibility is thin, and those who might be seen as set-ups. You can't always control what your references will say, but if you know them well and you have a good working relationship with them, you are in a good position. Be sure you ask your references if they mind being called on your behalf before you give their names.

Sometimes the interview process seems so extended that when an offer is made it almost seems anticlimactic. By this time, if you and the interviewers have been thorough, you probably have a pretty good picture of what the job entails, and they probably have a decent idea of how well you will be able to handle the work. Now the questions you have discreetly delayed putting forward can be discussed: How much money will you make? How much vacation time do you receive? Can you take it whenever you want? What other benefits are there? What about long hours? Since the shoe is on the other foot—the company wants you now—this is your time to bargain. Play your strengths here, because once you sign on the dotted line you will never again be in as good a bargaining position; but be realistic. Offers can be rescinded, for example, if it becomes clear that no meeting of the minds regarding salary is going to take place.

You are in the strongest position if you are not really desperate for a job. If you have a job you do not have to vacate, or if you have other offers, you can really hold out for what you want. The more you need the job, the less a prospective employer is likely to believe that you won't take a few thousand dollars less. A good increase in changing jobs is between 10 and 25 percent. A 5 percent increase is practically no increase at all because most salaries are increased by about that amount each year anyway. Salaries are usually negotiable within a range that the interviewer knows, but you don't. If you know something about the job market in your area, if you ask for a reasonable increase, if you can cite competing offers, you will probably get close to what you want. (You may even get more if the employer thinks someone else will win you with a higher bid.) Be sure to ask about profit-sharing and incentive programs. Additional subsidies can substantially increase your salary, but remember not to depend on these additional amounts because they are usually tied to profits or productivity.

MATCH-MAKING

Vacations are less negotiable, but there are usually industry standards and you can control your vacation time to some extent by the type of industry you select for your job search. Large commercial banks, for example, tend to be generous with vacation days, and in addition offer bank holidays. Small consulting firms, on the other hand, cannot do business if each of the few people in their employ take extended vacation leaves—especially if they all choose to go at the same time.

Other benefits—health care, retirement funds, etc.—are usually packaged equally for all employees of a certain level at the company, and are not really negotiable. Many companies, however, have flexible compensation packages that allow employees a choice about which types of benefits they wish to receive, and how much they wish to contribute to optional plans. It is wise to ask about retirement and health funds, vacation, and salary directly, and to get your answers in writing, especially if you are dealing with a small company. While most companies do not lie about these matters, some have been known to change the game plan after the candidate accepts the job and severs all other ties. Dishonest employers such as these usually rely on the fact that the employee will probably not go to the trouble of suing—especially if there isn't a commitment in writing—and that the employees will remain on the job anyway because they have nowhere else to go.

In the final analysis, while much of the job-hunting process seems to be luck—being in the right place at the right time— much of it is really up to the job-seeker. If you do your homework—assess your needs, consider your options, take a rational and consistent approach to your search, think out moves carefully, and give yourself time, you are likely to succeed.

Chapter 6
Ego Problems on the Slow Track

Even if you're determined—for a multitude of valid reasons—that in terms of interest and skills you belong on the "slow" track, and even though you know that this career path has many advancement opportunities and is valued by the organization in which you work, you still may find yourself, at one point or another, plagued by doubt about whether you made the right choice. How you cope with these doubts can add to or subtract significantly from your chances of success on the job.

If you are subject to doubt, it is important to remember that you are not alone. Most people—line or staff, new employees or veteran workers—feel doubt every now and then about what they are doing and how they are progressing. The kinds of questions that bother most employees are: Can I really do the work? Is the work valuable? Is it professionally fulfilling? Am I progressing fast enough? Will I get along with my co-workers and managers? And, particularly for staff people, am I a second-class citizen in this job?

CAN I REALLY DO THE WORK?

This is one of the questions recently hired employees most commonly ask themselves, particularly if they are beginning in a field or an organization, or are new to the job market. When you are first hired, you may be acutely aware that you lack specific knowledge about your new company—and maybe even about the business as a whole. In addition, you may have an underlying fear that you were hired to do something you cannot do, or that your job duties will never really become clear to you. It is natural to have these anxieties, but you should also view your fears in perspective. Usually, those who have hired you are convinced you can do the job because you have presented a full account of yourself and they feel your skills mesh with the requirements of the job; and they will try their best to make sure you understand what they want you to do.

When you first enter a company, there is generally an expectation that you will need time to adjust, time to learn the company, time to understand your duties. Your management should carefully explain your responsibilities, relate your responsibilities to those of the department as a whole, and introduce you to the people with whom you will interact. He or she should do so slowly and let you have time to assimilate your new knowledge. Your duties should be manageable, and they will be if your boss has thought out your position in advance. You will probably go to an orientation program; or be assigned a colleague who will help you get your feet wet; or spend a lot of initial time interacting with the boss.

If you are making an honest effort, energetically trying your best, asking questions when you are puzzled or confused, and attempting to learn as much as you can about the business through reading or conversations, you should find yourself feeling more secure after a few weeks on the job. Your "proving" period may be several months or even a year, but you should receive feedback—on small parts of your job—on a regular basis. You should not have to wait for your first annual review to find out how you're doing. If you get negative feedback as a result of a task you've completed, try to determine the reasons for it—ask the boss why—and express your willingness to try it again. Often it is more important to have a good attitude towards your efforts than it is to do everything right the first time. And don't forget to remind your boss from time to time that you are still relatively new on the job.

Sometimes a new hire is expected to hit the deck running. Work is thrown on your desk, and "proving yourself" means doing it like a veteran. In this situation, it is best to just roll up your sleeves and begin. Take a stab. Do what you can, then seek out friendly colleagues for feedback before giving the work back to your boss. When you finally do submit the work to your manager, do so with a remark such as, "I've taken a stab at this and prepared a first draft. I'd like you to look at it and tell me whether I'm on the right track and where it could be improved." Let your boss know in a positive way that *you* do not expect yourself to be the expert immediately, and neither should he or she.

IS THE WORK VALUABLE?

The old Groucho Marx line about not wanting to belong to a club that would have him for a member applies to business, too. Once employees feel confident about their abilities to do a certain job, they often begin to wonder whether the job is worth doing. Self-esteem is a very important part of job fulfillment; employees who do not think their jobs are worthwhile—or do not think their company values the work they are doing—are among the most discontented of staff members. There are ways to determine whether your function is vital or esteemed by your organization:

- *Do you or those to whom you report interact with senior management?* If you or your boss is doing work for some of the higher-ups in the firm, chances are the work is valuable to the company. Staff functions performed for the business's head are often the last to be cut. If you are writing speeches for the chairman, for example, your function will probably not be touched, even if speech writing is not a common job throughout the company. If the president feels the need for you to consider furniture and office space arrangement, it stands to reason that as long as he or she feels that way, your job will be secure.
- *Does your job contribute in any way to the "bottom line" of the company?* If you can trace your professional activities to any of the company's earning capacity, then you can be sure your function is considered important. If you do marketing communica-

tions, for example, and the products for which you have written brochures are making money, your job will most likely be considered vital. If you are a recruiter and the company has asked you to help increase sales by finding several new first-rate salespeople, you are in a good position in terms of your value to the company.

* *Do employees in other areas seem to respect you and ask you about what you do?* The attention of other workers is attracted by a winner, regardless of that person's department. Your fellow workers in areas other than your own will hear about your worth through the grapevine, and while the grapevine is not always accurate about reporting people in trouble, it is usually pretty much on target about people who are doing a good job. It is human nature not to waste much breath praising others, so if you sense that your colleagues, particularly those in different departments, respect you, you can be confident that you are valuable. Moreover, others want to be perceived as being friendly with a winner, so the approval of others is a fairly accurate hallmark of success.

Even if you sense that senior and line management, as well as colleagues, think your job is important, you still might not believe it. Recent studies have suggested that many people feel they are really not as valuable or successful as other people perceive them to be. They feel they are frauds and fear "discovery." If this is your feeling, it might help to let the respect of others guide your self-esteem. You might also consider that a little bit of self-doubt isn't necessarily bad—it might lead you to consider ways of improving your performance, even if what you are doing is basically OK to begin with.

IS THE WORK FULFILLING?

Related to the question of the value of your work to the organization is the question of the value of the work to you. The answer to this question is dependent on your own set of values.

You may, for example, feel that the most important work for society is being done in the public sector, and that your work in a profit-making company is not "socially useful." Or you may feel that what you are doing is not "creative" or "artistic" in any way. Or you may feel that you are underutilized and that you possess skills that are not being tapped in your job.

If you do not feel completely fulfilled by your work, remember that there are other options for socially useful or artistically interesting activities in your spare time. In this case, it would be best to choose a company that encourages its employees to have a complete range of activities outside of work. Some companies and many managers feel that employees perform better on the job if they are active and involved in family or community affairs. If you are employed by a company or boss who feels all your waking hours should be devoted to work, and this work is not personally fulfilling, you should probably consider transferring to another company.

You also might want to rethink your attitude towards your work or company if you do not feel fulfilled. It is possible that you are not seeing the value your company provides the community. Many an "artistic" or "creative" type has come to realize that his or her company provides support of art, education, community and health programs, and makes as much if not more contribution to society than many nonprofit organizations.

AM I PROGRESSING FAST ENOUGH?

Even if you find the work challenging and engaging, and you think your company is socially valuable, you still might worry about the speed of your own progress up the corporate ladder. It is human nature to believe that you are always in line for the next promotion, and to assume that you are destined for a high spot in the department or even the corporation. But even if you are a star, the odds of making it to the top—and making it quickly—are against you. Only a few make it all the way up the professional ladder. You can, and in most cases should, aim to go as far as you can. It doesn't hurt to dream of a rapid and stellar rise; but maintain your sense of reality and recognize that you can still be a success in your own eyes and the eyes of others even if you don't become a CEO.

FIRST, GIVE IT TIME

Do not expect your first promotion six months after your arrival. Look around you and try to determine how long promotions generally take in your area. Are people there a year? two? five? before they are moved up? Gauge your expectations by what usually happens. Next, try to figure out what those who have been promoted have done to deserve it. Have they been innovative? good team players? in thick with the boss? just lucky enough to be in the right place at the right time? Have they been there the longest? See what seems to work for most, then try to position yourself to take advantage of the trend.

While you should attempt to make generalizations about the progress of others in your group, don't make the mistake of comparing yourself to just one other person in your area—or worse, in another company. There are people who eat their heart out for years because their best friend or chief competitor is ahead of them on the corporate ladder and there is very little chance of catching up to or equalling the performance of this person. These people are foolish. For one thing, there are often hidden reasons for some people's success, such as accomplishments that are not publicly known, a special relationship to the boss, and many others. Measure yourself against the norm, not against one or two individuals. Give yourself enough time to achieve a logical next step. Then, if you still feel you are behind, reassess your position.

REASSESS, GIVE IN, OR GET OUT

If you really feel that you are not moving as fast as the average employee, that you are being passed over for promotions and salary increases, and that you do not have much to expect in the way of future career advancement, you have two choices: accept the fact that you have gone as far as you can in your field or company or look for greater advancement opportunities elsewhere.

WILL I GET ALONG WITH MY MANAGERS, CO-WORKERS, AND SUPPORT STAFF?

It is important to understand three things when you embark on a new job: you have to prove yourself on a personal level to your new bosses, you have to be accepted by your new colleagues, and you have to earn the respect and cooperation of your subordinates. Even though those who hired you probably would not have done so if they had not liked you and felt you would fit in, you still have to establish a working relationship with them to ensure that you are a comfortable and productive member of the team. And even though your new co-workers look at you with some interest and may appear friendly, you should remember that you are an unknown, and before they take you into the group completely you have to prove that you can be trusted and that you are not a threat to their own security or advancement. This is an especially tricky area because you do not know when you arrive whom you displaced, who wanted the job that you landed, and with whom you are competing for the next advancement. Moroever, you will surely have enormous difficulty succeeding if you do not earn the respect and cooperation of your secretaries and other subordinates.

A lot depends on you in successfully coping with the triple challenge of getting along with the boss, becoming accepted among your colleagues, and becoming a respected manager. While we will deal with these issues in greater depth in later chapters of this book, some general advice is in order here:

- *Be fair and pleasant to others.*   You are off to a good start if you exhibit and maintain a positive disposition, do not engage in gossip and backbiting, do not complain about people or conditions, and do your fair share of the work. If you are generally considered to be a cooperative team player who cares about the good of the organization and is not perceived as being solely out for personal gain, your fellow workers at all levels will consider you trustworthy and a valuable member of the group. Establish early on that you can be trusted, that you care about others, and that you are fun to be around, and you will find yourself in a very comfortable position.

- *Be careful about figuring out whom you can trust.* While you know that *you* are trustworthy, you do not know immediately whom on the staff you can confide in and trust. Don't plunge heedlessly into relationships where you reveal your own weaknesses or doubts. Get to know your fellow workers before you confide in them. You do not want to find the dirty linen you entrusted to someone else to take to the laundry hanging in public.
- *Maintain your integrity.* Shakespeare's line in *Hamlet,* "To thine own self be true," is as applicable in today's world as it was in the seventeenth century. In attempting to become an accepted member of the working group you are in, do not do or say anything that will compromise your own values, goals, or ideals. You will find that even if you are going against the common feeling, you will be respected for upholding your own point of view, and you will be appreciated more for your consistency than if you wavered and went along with the crowd. A job is only a job, and it is replaceable. Your self-respect and the true respect of others is not something that, once lost, can be easily replaced. And remember, most businesses have a sense of corporate integrity as well. Most companies work according to principles they believe in; and they will respect this quality in their employees.

AM I A SECOND-CLASS CITIZEN IN THIS JOB?

The above questions, while applicable to those holding staff jobs, apply equally to most business situations. The question of second-class citizenship, however, is really one of concern just to staff people.

The kinds of reminders of second-class citizenship you may receive range from snobbish remarks on the part of your "line" colleagues, to being in the first area required to reduce expenditures and staff during a budget crunch. Your reactions to such circumstances should involve two important considerations: keeping your ego intact, and determining whether your job or function is in any real danger.

If you are secure in your own mind about your reasons for working in a staff area, do not be bothered by insensitive remarks or attitudes on the part of line workers. If you like the work, the people, and the atmosphere, then what others say doesn't matter. You should know—and a successful company does know—the value that staff areas provide to corporations. Your department would not be in existence if the business did not think it worthwhile to fund your area.

If, on the other hand, your company itself is sending signs that it does not value your area—budgetary and employee cutbacks, lack of senior-level support or approval of most projects, lack of availability of senior managers to your department managers—then it is time to read the writing on the wall and begin to search for another job—this time in a company that places value on staff activity.

Ego problems plague everybody—line or staff. Try to keep your own in perspective: understand their origins, think out their solutions, learn to cope with your fears and worries, and you will find your job, your career, your future more secure.

Part III
Surviving and Thriving as a Staffer

Chapter 7
Starting to Move

Contrary to what many job-seekers think, landing a job doesn't mean the end of career planning. Many feel it is less difficult to land a good job than to keep it and make it increase in value once you have it. To plan—and stay on—a successful career path, you have to develop a strategy. Moreover, you should build an understanding of organizational behavior so you can avoid pitfalls and take advantage of opportunities. This chapter and the following one contain information that should help you to start up and keep going.

THE BASES FOR SUCCESS

Once you're on a company's payroll, there are several "musts" that are necessary for success:

BE PRODUCTIVE

Sometimes the reason you're hired is that you represent new blood. In this case, the more new ideas you can come up with and implement in your job, the more you'll be seen as Superperson, the prize worker snatched from the grasp of other corporations, who will help the company to clear the competition in a single bound.

Barry Blume was just such a superstar. An expert in marketing, with an MBA from a prestigious business school and an impressive list of publications in various marketing newsletters and journals, Barry was hired by a third-rate pharmaceutical firm at a very respectable salary, beating out a whole string of overqualified candidates, not because of his on-the-job experience, which was limited, but because of his brightness and ability to generate imaginative ideas. The firm's problems were not in the quality of their products, but in their ability to market these products in a competitive environment. The firm was taking a gamble; a more successful firm probably would have gone with someone with more experience than Barry had, but who might have been less imaginative. Their gamble paid off. Barry was an immediate success. His unique ideas about advertising, his gift for picking the right media through which to market the firm's products, and his willingness to put his job on the line and try new approaches struck just the right note and the company's sales started to climb. So did Barry's career.

Another winner whose ideas paid off was Ellen Barnard. An ex-academic whose specialty was French literature, Ellen brought to a communications job in a group health insurance firm a novel way of looking at communications. Primarily because she had no idea of what the "traditional" way of communicating was in her firm or any other, she answered the interviewer's questions about how she would approach certain communications problems by applying things she had learned as a researcher and teacher. The interviewer was impressed by her inventiveness, and so was her new boss. By the time Ellen learned the ropes and figured out how far her approach was from the norm, she was being acclaimed by her boss as a new standardbearer. Her freshness and eagerness also contributed to alleviating the stale spirit that had permeated the department before Ellen's arrival.

Developing new ideas is not always the way to go, however. New hires with new ideas are sometimes seen as a threat—to their peers, who may fear that the new kids on the block will advance faster than they will; to their bosses, who may see them as potential usurpers of their jobs and power; and to their staffs, who may resent new ways of doing things and fear that their own jobs are not secure because they don't know what the new bosses want. In such cases, it is wise for a new hire to let some of the innovative ardor cool, at least until he or she is accepted and trusted and no longer viewed as a threat or a maverick. While the new person actually may be a threat—and in reality, competition is very strong in the business world—it is best not to be perceived as one, since it is very difficult to succeed without the support of fellow workers.

Martin Benoit found this out the hard way. He entered a small human resources consulting firm as an assistant account executive, full of ideas about how to run the business. While many of his ideas were actually very good—a main interest of his was how to do things more efficiently—his manner of suggesting and implementing these ideas was so offensive to those around him that no one would cooperate with him, and before long Martin found himself on the job market—involuntarily. Though he was polite and deferential while interviewing for the job, after he was hired he began telling his boss that she was approaching problems in an old-fashioned way, and that he had figured out a better way in his last job; he repeatedly antagonized his peers by suggesting to the boss that they were inefficient at what they did; and he got no assistance from his staff because he criticized them for what he thought of as failures, and never praised the projects they handled well. Even his clients disliked him because he was arrogant and could not compromise on any issue. Even though they sensed he would be difficult to work with, the company had taken a chance on Martin because he seemed to be full of good ideas; but the chance didn't work out.

While it is obviously not good for your career if you have an abrasive personality, the reality is that some people are more obnoxious than others. If you suspect you are not very easy to get along with, do some self-assessment. Management specialist Harry Levinson, in an article in *Harvard Business Review,* provides some advice for the bright business executive with an abrasive personality. First, to help you assess whether you are abrasive, he asks some basic questions:

1. Are you condescendingly critical? When you talk of others in the organization, do you speak of "straightening them out" or "whipping them into shape?"
2. Do you need to be in full control? Does almost everything need to be cleared with you?

3. In meetings, do your comments take a disproportionate amount of time?
4. Are you quick to rise to the attack, to challenge?
5. Do you have a need to debate? Do discussions quickly become arguments?
6. Are people reluctant to discuss things with you? Does no one speak up? When someone does, are his or her statements inane?
7. Are you preoccupied with acquiring symbols of status and power?
8. Do you weasel out of responsibilities?
9. Are you reluctant to let others have the same privileges or perquisites as yourself?
10. When you talk about your activities, do you use the word "I" disproportionately?
11. Do your subordinates admire you because you are so strong and capable or because, in your organization, they feel so strong and capable—and supported?
12. To your amazement do people speak of you as cold and distant when you really want them to like you?
13. Do you regard yourself as more competent than your peers, than your boss? Does your behavior let them know that?[1]

He then suggests:

If you ask yourself the questions on this page and find that you answer three of them in the affirmative, the chances are that your behavior is abrasive to the people around you. If you answer six or more affirmatively, it takes no great insight to recognize that you have more problems than are good for your career. Of course, none of these questions taken by itself is necessarily indicative of anything, but enough affirmative answers may reveal an abrasive profile.

If you are the problem and it troubles you, you can work at self-correction. Most often, however, you need the help of a third person—your spouse, a friend, your boss, or a professional. If your behavior causes you serious problems on the job, then a professional is indicated. Managers and execu-

[1]Harry Levinson, "The Abrasive Personality," *Harvard Business Review* (May–June 1978).

tives with naturally heavy orientations to control, need to check themselves carefully for this kind of behavior lest unconsciously they defeat their own ends.[2]

If you have good ideas, and are easy to get along with or are working on making yourself so, it is still prudent to remember that easy success is not assured. Good ideas often fail. If you have an idea that bombs, don't forget that failure is not always fatal to a career. How you deal with it is often very important in keeping yourself on track. An article in Research Institute of America's *Personal Report* suggests that you "go out with style and candor. It could make heads turn and salvage for you a respect nor ordinarily gained from failure." The article suggests ways to do this:

To accommodate that possibility, here are five things to *avoid*—and the rest will take care of itself:

- *Don't count on time or money to bail out your brainchild.* Even when time isn't money, although it usually is, push away the temptation to use up more of it in the hope that, somehow, another few months may yet prove the idea a winner. Once you've exhausted a rational number of twists and turns and your bag of tricks is empty, time alone is rarely enough to breathe new life into a fast-fading project. To buy more time now is to risk looking worse later.

    Nor is money itself going to salvage you. It's horrible to think of, say, $200,000 going down the drain and easy to say, "Just another $50,000 and we'll turn the corner." When that temptation comes, remember Gresham's Law: "Bad money drives out good money."
- *Don't look to heaven.* When a once-promising idea begins to go to pieces and it becomes clear that it was a mistake, inertia sometimes sets in. The genius who started it all goes into a period of procrastination—a sort of look to heaven to deliver a miracle that will prove it was really workable all along.

    This only puts off the inevitable and rarely makes a manager look any better.
- *Don't look for a scapegoat.* Higher management is one of

[2]Ibid.

the favorites. "They bought the idea because I pushed hard, but they never really got behind it." There may be some truth in that—higher management may prevent a more serious disaster by withholding support at some point—but it's better left unspoken once the idea is clearly doomed. Looking for a scapegoat is always a weak move.

- *Don't look for blame-sharers.* After the flop of an idea or of a project that you originated and were in charge of, keep away from the collective "we." Don't drag subordinates or other managers working with you into the obituary. "We had a great thing going there for a while" or "Frank, Jerry and I were sure we had a winner" sounds okay—except that it wasn't their idea, but yours.

  It's to your credit that you were able to get others to join you and help you. It will be all the more to your credit if you separate them from the failure and take the rap alone.

- *Don't strain to look good.* Few things make executives look as bad as trying to look good while *really* looking bad. When your idea bombs and, inevitably, you're not appearing in the best light, so be it. Give people a chance to see you that way for a while. (It's often not as bad as you think anyway.)

The alternative faulty strategy is to run off in a couple of other directions in an effort to try to balance things out. It won't work. It may even accentuate the failure at the expense of the other things you're trying to accomplish. Better to save those things until the bright idea has had a decent funeral, then get to work on something more likely to survive and shine.

Observation: Three consolations to keep in mind:

1. There is no such thing as a total loss. Always there are lessons to be learned from failure that can lead to more successful ventures in the future.
2. Sometimes an idea that flops is merely launched on the world before its time—for example the telephone that was developed as an aid to the deaf and never made it in that market. There's a possibility—not probability, but possibility—that someday your brainchild, reshaped to meet the demands of a future day, could prove a winner

after all. But don't live on the hope—let it go completely for now.

3. It shows great and deserved self-confidence to say, "I used my best judgment, put in my best effort, but it just didn't work." That's the stuff of which the best executives are made.[3]

New ideas are not the only way to success. If your new job is not ripe for innovative ideas, make your mark by improving on old ones. Many an unimaginative professional has made a success by making minor improvements in the way projects are done. Chances are you're being hired to fill a position for which the necessity has been proven; if you attempt to change things radically, you may not accomplish what you were hired to do.

Esther Hernandez was a very steady achiever, but she was the first to acknowledge that she did not possess a vivid imagination. No one came to her when they needed a brilliant idea. Yet she rose consistently and rapidly in her career path as a promoter of special events for a bank because she instinctively recognized ways to cut waste, to streamline procedures, to take pieces of different projects and put them together in new and better ways. And she always took note of other people's successful ideas and incorporated them into her own projects.

MAINTAIN A POSITIVE ATTITUDE

In addition to ideas—new and improved—a necessary ingredient for success in most firms is a positive attitude. Say "yes" to almost everything, even if you really mean "I'll try even though it's not my job" or "I'll try although I don't think it will work." It's expected. You're staff. When you have to say "no," be sure your boss knows why (and be sure you have a good case).

Management specialist Arnold R. Deutsch, in his book *How to Hold Your Job*, has some sound advice about projecting a good image:

---

[3]"The Panorama Principle," *Research Institute Personal Report for the Executive,* 7, no. 16 (1981): 2–3. Reprinted with permission and copyrighted by The Research Institute of America.

The person who brings a positive attitude to a job has a better chance of climbing up the ladder and will likely perform more efficiently than will persons with negative or mediocre attitudes. While some workers, by their nature and experience, have better attitudes than others, good attitudes can be cultivated.

First, take pencil in hand and list the positive aspects of your job. Don't forget such items as opportunities for promotion, benefits, and co-workers, as well as free parking, proximity to home, and training opportunities.

Next, analyze your career goals. List the progress you have made since this time last year. Don't forget any raise you have had, new and more efficient tools furnished, or better working conditions provided.

Finally, list the people you have contact with on a daily basis at work. Beside each name write a phrase describing this person's greatest strength. For example: "Jim—helpfulness and patience; Gene—sense of humor; Mark—concern for his family; Evelyn—training ability."

Exercises such as these will help you understand your job and its benefits and will help you understand your co-workers and appreciate them. Understanding will help improve your work attitude.[4]

It is especially important that you project a positive attitude in a staff position because the nature of staff work is "service."

Susan Delano projected a positive image. She rose to middle and then upper management in a communications department because she never considered anything to be outside of the realm of her responsibility. She would as soon write a memo for her boss, type it and copy it, as she would do extensive research into an intricate problem. And she was pleasant about doing both. She showed such dependability that she became an indispensable member—and eventually the head—of the communications team. Another member of the same department, Claude Green, who was every bit as good at his job as Susan, was passed over several times for promotions because his boss did not think he pulled as hard for the team as Susan did.

[4]Arnold R. Deutsch, *How to Hold Your Job* (Englewood Cliffs, N.J.: Prentice-Hall, 1984), pp. 27–8.

Claude often refused assignments he considered below him or not part of his job description.

This is not to suggest that a staff member should fill his or her time with menial tasks that should and could be done by someone lower down in the hierarchy; but if certain less-than-elevated tasks appear in a project, they should not be shunned out of snobbishness. The most important thing you can do to further your career is get things done. If this means typing the outline yourself, then do it. If something has to be in an executive's office by four and the messenger service stops at three, then take it there yourself. If there's a small, low-visibility job to do along with a big, high-visibility one, don't overlook it in the rush to impress your boss. He or she may not notice it if you've done both, but if you don't do the little job, you can be sure he or she will remark on it. "Staff" means "service," and that's your prime responsibility.

DEVELOP YOUR REPUTATION AS A "STAFF SPECIALIST"

One strategy for getting ahead is establishing yourself as a specialist in your field. Whether you are a communicator or a recruiter, an office-space planner or a meal arranger, you should start to develop a trail of experience and accomplishments that makes you unique.

- *Constantly develop the skills that got you the job in the first place, and learn new ones.* Everyone's skills, no matter how good they are initially, can stand improvement. Practicing them day after day will certainly help, but that is not enough. It is important to learn from your mistakes and to accept constructive criticism from your peers and superiors. Too many people cannot swallow their pride enough to enable them to consider criticism without defensiveness. Certainly some criticism is unjustified; but if your work is subject to criticism, you should recognize that there may be some validity in it, and try to determine how your performance can improve. Ask for further explanations from those who comment on your work;

ask your personnel representative for advice if appropriate; look at similar work done by someone else and see what they are doing that you are not.

Professional courses and seminars in your area can help as well, as can current published books and articles. You can often learn about such courses through professional organizations in your field of work; in some corporations—large ones in particular—the human resources department provides additional training in the form of seminars and other courses.

Taking programs in areas related to but not exactly in your specialty—computer courses, for example—can expand your experience, complement your skill base, and make you more valuable as an employee if there are ways you can use your new skills at work. At times, learning new skills will help you think about your job or function in a new way, and this might enable you to provide the impetus for your department to move ahead into new areas.

- *Learn the business of the company you are in.* This is of extreme importance. Having well-developed technical skills is only valuable insofar as you can use these skills to further the work of your company. Knowing how to write and edit articles and speeches, for example, is a valuable set of skills for a bank's communications department only if you are also conversant with the business of banking. If, because of your technical skills, you have been hired into a certain business area that is not familiar to you, lose no time in learning the ropes. Read all you can about the business; talk to people; take courses. The initial grace period when people still consider you "new" will be short-lived, and you will find that you will be expected to be conversant about the business quite quickly. If you appear "new" too long, you may find yourself back on the job market.
- *Develop your network of professional peers outside your company.* This is important not only because

you might need these peers from time to time as contacts for initiating a job search, but because it is important to develop a reputation in your firm as a respected member of a profession. In addition, keeping abreast of developments in your field will help you do your job better. Join professional organizations, read their material, participate in their activities, and know what's new in your area.

- *Establish solid achievements in your line of work outside the marketplace.*   Using your skills for special projects such as writing books and articles, or for volunteer work, or for some freelance work will impress your management with your professionalism, and will keep you looking at your work in fresh ways. As long as you avoid conflicts of interest, and as long as your extracurricular work doesn't take away from time at work or time doing business, most employers like you to be involved in other professional and voluntary activities. They are aware of the extra dimensions such work gives employees.
- *Remain flexible in developing yourself as an "expert."*   Never become so specialized that any variance from the "old ways" of working leaves you looking like an anachronism. Make sure that your skills and knowledge base cover a wide range; keep up with changes; know where your company and industry are headed and learn about these new areas; and keep restructuring your resume so that what you have done in the past can be positioned to suggest what you will be able to do in the future.
- *Please your audience.*   One of the biggest frustrations of a service job is that you have to please a multiplicity of audiences. You have to gain your boss's approval, you have to maintain your credibility and productiveness in the eyes of the company's hierarchy, and you have to satisfy your client. This is very important for career success, and deserves further comment.

PLEASING YOUR AUDIENCE

MANAGING THE BOSS.
_____

In some ways, pleasing your boss is the easiest of the three tasks. He or she is usually one person; it is possible (though sometimes tricky) to figure out what he or she wants you to do, and then to learn to do it, or to get around it. Remember: it is feasible to succeed in your job even if you don't get along with your boss.

There is much helpful advice in management literature about getting on the good side of your boss: begin with a genuine respect for him or her if you can; play from his or her strengths; work to put him or her in the best light possible; flatter him or her and show your respect by accepting his or her ideas and suggestions when they are good ones, and by discussing those with which you disagree; avoid showing him or her up; don't surprise him or her by presenting results to a client without first obtaining his or her approval; eschew any activity that is disloyal or sneaky.

Various personnel and management experts have written extensively on these topics and others. In one of the most intelligent articles on this subject, "How to Manage Your Boss," Peter F. Drucker gives this advice:

> If there's one problem most of us talk about, grumble about, but do nothing about, it's the boss. Every manager I know finds managing the boss the most difficult task he has. Very few even try.
>
> How you handle the problem of your boss can be quite revealing. For example, it is one of the few indicators we can rely on to tell which of the younger people in an organization are going to go places and which are going nowhere. Those who only talk about how incompetent and impossible the boss is and complain about how much they suffer are not going anyplace. On the other hand, you can spot the comers because they do something about managing the boss—and I don't necessarily mean buttering him up or polishing the apple. It's really quite simple. What you do almost depends on the boss himself.

- The first thing to recognize is that the boss is neither a monster nor an angel; he's a human being who insists on behaving like one. Bosses, therefore, have to be treated like human beings, like individuals. So for some bosses, then, you do polish the apple; for others, that's the worst thing you can do.
- The second thing to know is that no matter how able and competent the boss is, he is not a mind reader. You have to make sure he understands what you're trying to do.
- The third thing to remember is that although he does not give you enough of his time, he gives more, as a rule, than he should—more than he has to give. So it's up to you to manage that time and to ensure that it's productive time.
- Finally, remember that it's more dangerous to underrate the boss than to overrate him. The most serious mistake you can make is to underrate the boss and be caught doing it.[5]

Other experts offer additional advice. An article in *New England Business* on a seminar given by business professor Bob Mezoff also suggests ways to handle the boss:

The strategies of boss handling can be fairly basic. Mezoff cited some:

- Know the boss's strong and weak points. On things that the boss hates to do, "work like the devil" to gain mastery of the field so the boss can be relieved of it. If the boss doesn't like to make presentations, offer to handle these for him or her.
- Know what the boss's goals are. Subordinates who don't have a clear idea of the boss's goals are headed toward a "potentially catastrophic situation," said Mezoff. A 1980 article in the *Harvard Business Review* (used by Mezoff as a seminar handout) cites the case of a top-notch marketing manager hired as a vice president for a company that had been acquired by a larger corporation. His ostensible job was to "straighten out the marketing and sales problems." He didn't realize—because he didn't try to clarify

[5]Reprinted with permission from Peter F. Drucker, "How to Manage Your Boss," *Management Review,* May 1977, pp. 8–9.

what his boss's objectives were—that improving sales was just *one* of the president's goals. Both the president and the vice president wound up fired.

- Don't get hung up on the boss's mannerisms or petty traits that seem annoying. Accept bosses as human beings with frailties and shortcomings; regard frustrating, aggravating traits as insignificant.
- If the boss is the kind who doesn't get ulcers but gives them, don't approach such people and say you don't like them blowing their stack. The strategic move, said Mezoff, would be to find them on a day when they're calm and say, "It's really a pleasure to work with you when you're calm because I feel we get much more accomplished and I enjoy our relationship much more." This kind of strategy is immensely powerful. People do respond to that kind of reinforcement. If you continue to give praise or psychological strokes any time that you catch them doing something good, you will continue to see greater and greater repetition of behavior that you like.[6]

On another side of this subject, the publication of the International Association of Business Communicators suggests how to say "no" to the boss:

A communications professional, on occasion, must take a stand if a superior's request is contrary to the norms and standards of the profession or contrary to personal values. This doesn't require standing on a moralistic soapbox or even risking your job if some of the following strategies can be used:

- Appeal to self-interest. Tell the boss that he or she will lose credibility and the esteem of colleagues if the current plans are not modified. If the person is in line management, point out how dissemination of the information may jeopardize the company's reputation.

---

[6]Barbara W. Carlson, "Managing the Boss Is Easier Than You Might Think," *New England Business* 4, no. 14 (1982). Material from Robert Mezoff, "How to Manage Your Boss,", Seminar, reprinted with permission from ODT Associates, P.O. Box 134, Amherst, Mass. 01004.

- Suggest a compromise. In most cases, if the superior has any respect for your expertise and ability, you can suggest an alternative that satisfies your specific concerns.
- Excuse yourself from the project. Express your personal or professional concerns about the specific project. Request that you be reassigned to another project where you could do a better job devoid of personal conflicts. In most cases, the superior will respect your wishes and give the assignment to another person in the office. This tactic has even been known to get people a salary increase because the superior is impressed with their honesty and professionalism.
- If in the U.S., cite Federal Trade Commission or Securities Exchange Commission regulations. Misleading the public about a product or hyping the financial health of a company can cause the employer extensive and expensive legal problems.
- Cite the corporate code of conduct. Many companies have a published code of conduct that provides guidelines for the business conduct of all employees. The courts have ruled that employees who violate published codes and company standards can be fired.
- Invoke the IABC[7] or PRSA[8] code of ethics. Professionalism means allegiance to the standards and norms of the profession. By citing a published code, it adds weight to your arguments.
- File a lawsuit. If you do get fired over a matter of professional ethics, sue for unjust and illegal dismissal. Loyalty to an employer and insubordination is one thing; being asked to do things that are clearly illegal, unethical and contrary to the public interest is another matter.[9]

All this advice is to the good, but the most helpful action you can take to ensure your boss's approval is to like and respect him or her—and show it. Even when you thoroughly disagree

[7]International Association of Business Communicators
[8]Public Relations Society of America
[9]Dennis L. Wilcox, "Saying No to the Boss," *IABC Communication World,* (November 1984): 17

with an approach to a project he or she suggests and have an approach of your own instead, discuss your ideas with your boss honestly and as respectful colleagues. Chances are you can win your point.

For example, Audrey Thomas began her career at a major automobile importing firm convinced that a particular marketing method was better than the approach her company was taking. Her boss, the head of marketing and sales, was responsible for the old way; although his method had been valid for years, Audrey thought, other companies were pulling ahead because they were using innovative and modern approaches to various marketing problems. Audrey was savvy enough to gain her boss's confidence before making her move to change her company's approach. She spent months successfully doing the job he outlined for her, and she made sure *he* knew she respected his knowledge, experience, and ways of doing things. Then she began introducing her new ideas gradually and informally; she presented these ideas as concepts on which she wanted his opinion. When the decision finally came to try some of these new-fangled approaches, the boss neither knew nor cared whether these ideas had originated with himself or with his subordinate. He was convinced that, though his methods were good, there might be ways of making an even better showing; and, with a basis of confidence on which to build, he was willing to try.

When considering the question of dealing with the boss, it is wise to remember that not all bosses deserve to be where they are, or are good at being top dog. If you find yourself in a situation where your boss is weak, on the way out, or unbalanced in some way, you will have to develop strategies to handle these situations. Drucker makes some suggestions about dealing with these problems in the article quoted previously:

> One of the first things to learn about managing anything is when to abandon it—even a boss. There's no better prescription for success than to have a boss who is going places, and there is no more certain prescription for frustration and failure than to work for an incompetent.
> Another time to change jobs is when the boss is corrupt.

He doesn't have to have his hand in the till—that's only one form of corruption. A more serious form of corruption is when the boss has values and standards that are ethically and morally unacceptable to you. Never work for a boss whose standards demean you—you become corrupt yourself, you become contemptuous of yourself, you begin to loathe yourself.

When it becomes obvious that you are working for an incompetent or corrupt boss, I think you have to say, "All right, I like the company, but this isn't going to work out." Abandon the job and look for something else—within the company or outside it.

You also have a problem if the boss is a paragon. It's possible to stay too long with a paragon or near-paragon for the good of your career. Staying makes it too easy to become just an 'assistant to' rather than your own man.

There's still a great deal of fear—though less now than ten years ago—of becoming the organization man, someone whom the organization uses as a servant. There has never been enough emphasis on the opposite, however; that is, looking upon the organization as *your* tool.

Size up your job from two viewpoints: (1) What can I contribute to it? and (2) What can it contribute to me? Also ask yourself, "What has it done for me lately?" and "What is it likely to do for me in the future?"

If you are in a position where you have gotten as much out of the job, the boss, and the company as they will ever give you and if you are still below late middle age and have given all you are likely to give, then it's time to move on. Don't move out too often, however, and don't rush. Remember there is a time limit, and keep in mind that a person moves out because of success as much as failure.[10]

Most often employee/boss relationships are pretty straightforward: the boss manages a group or function that serves a specific purpose in the company. The boss decides who does what and the employees perform their assigned tasks or manage their areas of responsibility. But at other times the division of responsibility is less defined, especially if the employee is

[10]Drucker, "How to Manage Your Boss," p. 12.

billed as a "special assistant to," and this vagueness can cause employees either to overstep their areas of responsibility or to underachieve. In such cases, it is best to keep the lines of communiation open between you and your boss and to keep asking questions about your responsibilities when they are unclear. Be as open as possible with the boss so you know when he or she thinks you are doing too much or too little. An article in *Research Institute Personal Report for the Executive* offers further suggestions for establishing the balance between doing too much and too little in an ill-defined professional situation:

- *Concentrate on perennial problems.* Every operation has some inefficiencies—bottlenecks, outmoded or cumbersome procedures, etc. Usually people have become so accustomed to them that they take them for granted; probably don't even wonder any more if there is a better way. Since nobody is actively engaged in trying to eliminate these headaches, you can take responsibilities without invading anyone else's territory. And since you are looking at the situation from a fresh perspective, you can probably come up with some improvements. If these make life easier for people, they will probably be welcomed—and you'll begin building a reputation as a good administrator.
- *Expand assignments into responsibilities.* When you are asked to do a specific task, think about what you could do to turn that area of activity into a permanent part of your job. For example, suppose your boss asks you to interview a clerical job applicant. You might interpret that as a request to interview all applicants and weed out those obviously not suited to the job. If you do that successfully, it is a relatively small step to becoming the person who handles clerical hiring for the operation, even if the task is never formally assigned.
- *Complement the boss's weaknesses.* Like everyone, your boss is a combination of strengths and weaknesses. Undoubtedly, there are aspects of the job that he or she dislikes. Attendance at certain routine meetings, for instance, could be one such activity, and you could offer to fill in on these. Or the boss may be uninterested in certain routine reports that have to be prepared. No reason why you can't draw up a rough draft for the boss to polish. If

your work is competent, pretty soon the boss's review will become perfunctory or even unnecessary.

- *Learn your boss's style.* Your boss's secretary can usually clue you in on any special preferences or idiosyncracies—for example, that the boss hates to be disturbed while reading the morning mail. You might find out whether the memos you send to your boss are really read, or if a verbal presentation would be more effective.

  Or, if written matter must necessarily be presented, you can learn beforehand whether your boss prefers a complete report with all the supporting technical data, or whether he or she would rather have a summary and recommendations and ask you about technical supporting data only as necessary.

- *Observation:* Some bosses have a very clear idea of what they want an assistant to do, but many more expect their second-in-command to take some burden off their backs without their having to go to the trouble of explaining how it should be done. Becoming a valued helper to the latter kind of boss requires exercising initiative, patience and interpersonal skills—all the while maintaining a low profile."[11]

MANAGING THE COMPANY'S HIERARCHY

Pleasing a company's hierarchy is trickier. Staff workers often have no personal contact with those who manage their company or firm at the highest levels and therefore have no chance to build credibility through interpersonal skills. And they often have no idea what the goals of senior management are. In addition, those at the top often do not agree among themselves as to what their mission or aims are. To please the hierarchy—and help keep the company on track—staff people often have to rely on the judgment of those to whom they are directly responsible, frequently middle managers.

Many staff people interact directly with senior members of a

[11]"Developing Your Skills as an 'Assistant To,' " *Research Institute Personal Report for the Executive* 8, no. 5 (1982): 3–4. Reprinted with permission and copyrighted by The Research Institute of America.

firm or corporation, and in these cases it is, of course, imperative that the worker please his or her senior management client. In many cases it just doesn't pay to worry about pleasing any of the company's hierarchy except your own boss. He or she is the one writing your reviews, deciding on your salary increases, and generally seeing to your future in the organization. In some cases, however, it can be of benefit to have the support of a manager high up in the company.

Having a mentor—your boss or another high-level manager—can be very important during your tenure at a particular company. Many an otherwise average employee has achieved stardom because of the support of a corporate mentor. If this supporter is your own boss, his or her rise can mean corresponding advancements for you as an invaluable contributor. If he or she is someone even higher than your boss, your mentor can intercede and hasten your rise in the company.

Of course, all this is dependent on the success of your mentor. If he or she fails, you may suffer along with him or her as the devoted protégé of a discredited regime. There are other pitfalls, as well. Another article in *Research Institute Personnel Report for the Executive* suggests what they are:

- *Expect to be envied.* This is an obvious hazard for anyone who has been singled out. And if the day comes when the protégé is raised to a higher rank, it can make it difficult to get the cooperation of those who were bypassed.

    A likable personality, good manner and, especially, demonstrably strong capabilities go a long way toward keeping the natural envy of others from becoming vituperative. But you may also have to be much shrewder than your mentor at judging the political climate of the organization. Top executives often feel that their sponsorship alone will be sufficient to protect lower-level managers whose careers they want to advance. Yet this won't necessarily be true at all times.

- *Keep your ears open.* If colleagues or executives on levels between you and your sponsor are obviously envious, you have a handy excuse for shutting out what they have to say. Anything which you would rather not hear can easily be written off as sour grapes.

But if you let that happen, then you are brushing aside opportunities to learn. While this is always harmful, it can become particularly so if, because of your mentor, you are promoted to a job for which you are really not well-trained and need all the ideas and constructive criticism you can get.

- *Mark off your independence as much as possible.* The protégé-sponsor relationship can become very much like that of a parent and child—with the result that the younger person may turn into a replica of the "parent," losing the ability to respond to situations which the mentor has never handled. In a world of rapid change, this rigidity has ruined the careers of some managers who seem to have everything going for them—including well-placed parent figures.

It isn't easy to stand up to someone you respect who also holds the key to your future. But there will be times when your judgment *will* be best and you will have to stick with it. And you'll also have to remain aware, in your own mind, of the distinction between your sponsor's goals and yours: They are bound to differ in some respects.

- *Don't become wedded to your mentor's career.* Moving to another organization with an older executive usually means advancement at a far faster pace than if you were to work your way up in the original company. But there are three potential dangers: 1) if the sponsor doesn't work out, you too will probably be asked to leave; 2) it may be impossible for you ever to rise above your mentor's level, at least until the executive retires; 3) when that day comes and you are ready to step into the job you've been coached for, you may find that the top brass has other ideas.

So before making such a move, consider whether you are being wooed with promises that your sponsor may not be able to deliver. You may decide to take the chance anyway. But if you do, be sure to find ways in your new job to make your own mark as an executive.

Above all, avoid appearing as though your major ability lies in bolstering your mentor's ego. Bear in mind that you can fall from this executive's grace without the world's coming to an end. In the long run, it is better to lose favor than to turn into a toadying courtier to whom work becomes a pastime, far less important than the need for constant politicking.

In fact, if it gets to the point where the relationsihp is no longer beneficial to *you*—and it won't be if you lose your pride and self-respect—be hard-headed about it. Get out while you still can call your soul your own.

Observation: Despite the pitfalls, it is generally foolhardy for a manager to reject the sponsorship of a higher-up. The traps are certainly there. But anyone who relies on performance to build both self-esteem and a solid basis for advancement, who maintains a sense of humor and of proportion and who doesn't let the friendship get in the way of less-exalted relationships can usually manage to have the best of both worlds.[12]

DEALING WITH CLIENTS

Pleasing your client is at times the hardest trick of all; and since most staff jobs have clients of some kind—whether they are internal or external, one person or many—it is essential to your career to know how to manage them. The most important thing to remember is that these clients are paying your salary, either directly or indirectly, and that without their projects you would be unemployed; therefore, what they want, goes. This isn't to say that when you have good ideas you shouldn't politely present them as "alternatives" to be considered. Just remember that your opinion should not be set in stone. The customer isn't always right, but the customer *is* always the customer.

Mattie Felder made the fatal mistake of putting quality ahead of everything else. She worked for a consulting firm that did human resources projects for companies. One of her clients was a new—and reluctant—buyer of her firm's services. He had written a draft of a recruiting brochure which Mattie was given to edit and then produce. The draft was poorly organized and written, and Mattie did a herculean job of editing and reorganizing, returning to the client a draft which was much better

[12]"Pitfalls of the Protégé," *Research Institute Personal Report for the Executive* 6, no. 15 (1981): 1–2. Reprinted with permission and copyrighted by The Research Institute of America.

written and very different from the original. But Mattie hadn't considered that the client's ego was very much wrapped up in the writing. What he wanted was a light edit ,and production. What he got was a piece of writing he could not call his own, and which he did not feel was representative of his company's image. The consulting firm for which Mattie worked had failed to make it clear to Mattie that they were trying to win the client's confidence and that though their ultimate aim was to try to improve the quality of the client's product, their first aim was to handle a project to the client's satisfaction. Mattie was too insensitive to recognize her client's ego or to anticipate his reaction to a rewrite of his material that implied he was lacking in writing skills. He immediately dropped the agency, giving as a reason that they did not do what he had asked them to do. Mattie's own career suffered a setback as a result of this incident. She was not fired, because her managers realized that they were partly at fault for not keeping her better informed of their goals, but she was thenceforth required to show everything she did to two levels of her firm's management before giving work to a client.

A staff worker should, of course, have standards about his or her work, but these standards should be exercised with some judgment and tact if the service agency wants to maintain a customer base.

In the above situation Mattie should have first sought advice from her own management concerning the amount of change it would be politic to make in the manuscript, then sat down with the client in an exploratory way to determine how attached he was to the piece. A good disarming opening question might have been, "I haven't really concentrated on the manuscript yet; do you think it's in pretty good shape as it is, or are you looking for some heavy editing?" Mattie would probably have picked up some clues from her client's answers to this query. She should then have gone along with her client's wishes and limited her changes to style, not content or organization.

If, after discovering her client's commitment to his own draft, Mattie still felt the need to make extensive stylistic changes, she might have negotiated her way into having the client accept at least some of them by saying, "This was really a very well-written draft and was very intelligently organized. I limited my edits to matters of style—consistency and format only." Most clients sensitive about their material only have to hear the words "well-done" and "intelligent" to get the feeling that the editor is on their side. And most people would welcome the opportunity to improve the superficial aspects of the work so it matches the quality of the basic ideas and concepts. It is much easier for a client to think, "I was so busy with the ideas I didn't have time to worry about grammar details; those superficial aspects of writing are the editor's job anyway," rather than, "This person—who's only an editor—thinks my ideas are stupid!"

Project managers like Mattie should always be willing to back off—even on stylistic matters—if the client really insists on doing it his or her way.

If in the rare event that a standoff occurs because of a disagreement involving the presentation of material that is dishonest or pernicious in some way, the staff person has no choice but to dissociate him or herself from the job completely. A firm with integrity should never compromise morals to please a client.

AVOID PITFALLS

To be perceived as one destined to get ahead, you need the approval and support of your boss, your peers, your subordinates, and those with whom you interact outside your department, either as colleagues or clients. The best way to ensure success is—as we previously mentioned—to know your job and do it well, and to make a big effort to get along with others. In addition, however, there are pitfalls to avoid:

- *Pay attention to details.* Remember that small errors count as much as, and sometimes even more than, big ones. And they're easier to make. Take the case of a young, ambitious, energetic administrative assistant in a prestigious accounting firm. She took on more than her share of difficult projects, working long hours and producing excellent and flawless results. She was very much at ease in the corporate world and seemed competent and destined for advancement until one day she slipped on a small detail and put the wrong date on a memo. The memo—though unimportant in itself—was widely circulated; her boss was mortified; and the administrative assistant was thenceforth known as sloppy and careless, despite the fact that this was literally her only mistake and the pressures of her work could certainly be seen as extenuating circumstances.

- *Never show your underbelly.* Offer no personal information that could be twisted around and used against you. When you begin to achieve success in your job, you can be sure that one of your colleagues or subordinates will fish out that piece of information you let slip over a drink one night and use it against you. Eddie Miller, for example, made the mistake of confiding to a colleague—his current "best" friend—that sometimes he was nervous when talking to high-level management, a seemingly understandable foible. His friend "understood completely," though he didn't have that problem, and took the next opportunity to confide to his boss, who was also Eddie's boss, that he was concerned about Eddie. He had observed that Eddie was so nervous his hands shook whenver he had to deal with a senior manager. The friend asked the boss's assistance in helping Eddie to overcome this problem. The friend also knew that both he and Eddie were being considered for a higher position, a position with more senior-management interaction. While he, too, often had butterflies in his stomach when approaching a senior offical, his "concern" for Eddie's problem ensured him the job.

Eddie's problem was that he was too trusting. A similar situation can occur if a person is naive. Kathleen Weber, for example, wasn't used to playing corporate games when she returned to work after her two small children were in school. She had always been open about her needs and goals, and this trait had always paid off in the past. So, after landing a job in human resources—a field she had worked in before having children—at a large media firm in New York, she assumed complete forthrightness was the right step. A mother with children, she knew, could not be discriminated against in the marketplace, and since she intended to work hard, she saw no reason to change her attitude towards truthfulness.

Kathleen worked hard and fast and efficiently, and her results were praised by her employers. But, while she stayed late and came in early when her job demanded it, in general she kept her hours nine-to-five so that she could take care of her family needs in the evening. She also knew that her colleagues never stayed more than fifteen minutes late or came in more than ten minutes early in the morning. The difference was that they talked about their huge workload and long hours, while she did not complain and stated quite openly that she could do all her work between the opening and closing of the business day.

She noticed the hostility gradually. Colleagues began making snide remarks in front of her boss about working "half-time." Her boss often left her messages when he got in at five to nine in the morning and called her at quarter after five, immediately before he left. It didn't seem to matter that she did her job well. What counted was that she foolishly admitted something that other people kept hidden: she openly stated that the workload was doable. Lured by her own determination to be "honest," she didn't realize she was violating a cultural norm. Regardless of the truth of the situation, others in her department either thought or wanted others to think they worked exceedingly hard; anyone who implied otherwise was either a phony or was trying to show them up, and would be treated as a pariah.

Kathleen's worklife became so uncomfortable that she soon began searching for another job. When she left the media firm, she still didn't know whether her old colleagues and boss honestly felt she wasn't pulling her weight, or whether they were jealous that she could get the job done and still find time for a family. Whatever the real reason, she decided not to be so ingenuous in her new job.

It's bad enough to contend with the occasional vicious corporate liar when the next rung of the ladder is at stake without giving such people ammunition.

- *Try not to give up an area of responsibility, or to volunteer for a job which someone lower on the pecking order can do.* For example, though you might find yourself doing the petty details of your own job, never volunteer to type anything for anyone else if typing isn't your job. Not only will you find yourself doing such favors for everyone, but you will suddenly find yourself labeled a clerical. (There are times when you might choose to lend a hand in a tough situation by doing a menial task that isn't assigned to you, but in this case be sure it is perceived as "pitching in in a pinch and being a team player" by others.)

Penny Rapp landed a job in the public relations department of a large midwestern manufacturing firm—the first woman to be employed by that department in any capacity other than secretarial. She was supposed to write press releases. There were no personal secretaries in the department because the office had recently gone "electronic" and all the press writers had individual word processors on which they were supposed to do their writing. It made sense economically. The department's only secretary was supposed to keep the supplies replenished, answer phones, etc., but not to type releases. Penny was a good typist and had typed her own papers and materials for years, so this situation posed no problem for her. Besides, she thought everyone did it. But her fellow writers—all men—resented the "loss of prestige" doing their own typing seemed to entail, especially since they always used to have personal secretaries to type their releases.

Penny's downslide began the day she agreed to do a "favor" for one of her fellow press-release writers who was "really busy" and was "such a slow typist" that he'd "never make the deadline" without her help. It only took twenty minutes and Penny really thought she was helping the department; but one "favor" led to another, and before too long Penny was doing everybody such favors and was finding it necessary to stay late and cut corners on her own writing to get everything done. The quality of her releases went down, and she was assigned fewer and fewer of them, so her productivity looked less impressive than that of her colleagues, who were actually producing more releases because of Penny's help. Her boss, who really didn't care who did the work or in what configuration as long as it got done well, rewarded the biggest producers and was not aware of Penny's problem. Her own polite and somewhat self-effacing personality made things worse, and when she finally mustered up the courage to tell her boss, he was as angry with her for allowing herself to be a lackey as he was with the others for taking advantage of her. A restatement of work duties by the boss helped in this case, but Penny's credibility as a productive press writer, as well as of her self-esteem, suffered because of the incident. She should not have given up responsibility.

- *The same goes for giving up space or subordinates.* If you lose a work area or a position that reports to you, whether you agreed to drop it to help the corporation or not, you become a smaller manager. There are times when you are forced to do such things, and in situations like these it is best to be gracious; but if you have a choice, maintain your ground. It's harder to get it back than to keep it.
- *Maintain your authority without losing your humanness.* For example, Ella Binger was young, bright, and good-natured and thrilled to be one of the youngest insurance salespeople in a solid firm. She was on cloud nine when she arrived at her new office

and found that she had her own secretary. Unsure of how to manage a secretary, Ella was reluctant to *tell* the secretary to do anything—primarily for fear of hurting her feelings. She was apologetic and equivocal whenever she gave an order, and soon her secretary, who was used to a firmer boss, began ignoring her. Bad went to worse and the secretary started to talk back, and then to talk about her boss to other salespeople.

In this case, the secretary became so obstreperous and so unproductive that she was fired for not performing up to the standards set for the job; but in some instances, particularly in large corporations, it is very difficult to fire someone if he or she has a generally good work record. And besides, in a case like this, the reputation of both the secretary and the boss is tarnished. The take home lesson is to believe in your own authority and convey it to others.

Learning to delegate effectively is one of the hardest things to achieve in working your way up the corporate ladder. Though we will spend more time on this subject in chapter 9, "When You Become a Manager," you should begin to think about this subject early in your career, and to practice it where possible.

There are several basic points to remember:

- As you attain more and more responsibility, it will become impossible for you to do everything yourself. You will have to learn to prioritize your activities so that you can determine which activities would represent more productive use of your time if you did them yourself, and which would make sense to let someone else do. If you do not have authority to delegate and you feel you need to do so, negotiate the problem with your boss and try to achieve either the right to hire a support staff, or the right to limit your project load.
- You should begin the delegation process when you think about hiring staff or filling subordinate positions. Always hire people that you trust and that you

know can do the job. If you do not think a subordinate is capable, you will be unable to delegate work you think is important.

If you are hired into a position with a subordinate staff already in place, assess their capabilities as quickly as possible (*before* you accept the job, if feasible) so you know what you can delegate safely and what you can't.

- Remember that you are still responsible for what you delegate. A subordinate's error is really your error, and you will be blamed for allowing it. If a subordinate is incapable of doing his or her job, move him or her to another area of responsibility, or terminate employment if possible. Be sure you check all your subordinates' work thoroughly, even if the staff is generally reliable; and be sure you clearly and completely convey to them your expectations about a project.

  Authority is important, but it does not give you license to be rude or excessively demanding in fulfilling your role. Little is accomplished when subordinates—secretaries or other workers—hate or fear their bosses. Loyalty is not established; an enjoyable work environment is not created; and productivity generally diminishes.

  Babette Deakins is a case in point. Petulant, demanding and critical, she quickly alienated all subordinates, both professional and clerical. Because she was a disorganized manager, she made unreasonable demands on her staff, often to cover up her own weaknesses—demands which a happier staff might have tried to meet. Her staff rebelled, individually approaching their human resources representative and asking for a transfer to another department. The emerging pattern was sufficient to alert Babette's own boss that the situation was getting out of control, and though he didn't fire Babette, he did not promote her to the next managerial level and Babette eventually left the company.

- Finally, be discreet. Gossip, tempting as it is to

engage in, can be fatal in the professional world. The less you gossip, the more you will be trusted and the fewer enemies you will incur. And the more you are trusted and liked, the easier it is to succeed.

Manny Kessler, for instance, simply refused to backbite. Although he was part of a sizable and highly competitive group of young men and women in a systems training program at a large prestigious corporation, Manny tried not to listen to or spread compromising tales of any sort. Moreover, he shrugged off what others in his set considered "insults" that had to be responded to in kind. His behavior soon netted him friends among his peers, since they knew he wouldn't turn against them, and it also earned him the respect of his supervisors, who noticed his behavior and gave him the credit he deserved for his maturity and fine character. As a result, though Manny was neither more clever nor better at his work than his colleagues, when a managerial position became available Manny was chosen to fill it. Manny certainly had adequate skills in his field, but that in itself would not have distinguished him from his peers nor ensured his rapid rise within the company's systems department.

Getting a good start in your career means that if you've chosen wisely and there is a career path for you, success if attainable. Being productive and avoiding pitfalls, exercising your finest interpersonal skills, and being savvy about the attitudes you assume are all essential in accomplishing your career goals—whether in staff or in line positions.

Chapter 8
Strategies for
Keeping Up
the Momentum

The question of how to move ahead both in good times and during a crunch faces everyone, line or staff, at one time or another during his or her career. It is a concern of management as well as of each individual employee. Most major firms give at least lip service to a commitment to career development; some even have departments or programs to ensure career pathing. These programs encompass everything from education and training for promising—and nonpromising—employees to early identification and development of "stars." All this is to the good. It benefits an organization to have a reputation of encouraging good people to progress quickly, and it builds morale and productivity among its employees.

Most managers find little difficulty in promoting subordinates to higher levels—as long as they remain subordinates and as long as their levels are lower than the manager's. However, rare indeed is the boss who is so altruistic he or she encourages an employee to be raised to a level equal to or above his or her own level, or promotes an employee right out of his or her department. It is unrealistic to assume most managers will say, "My employee is doing well in my department and the whole department looks good because of him. Therefore, let's get him into a more important job in another department." The manager's department will suffer for the loss of this employee, and the manager's ego will suffer by seeing a subordinate gain on him or her. A recent issue of *"The Levinson Letter,"* a management publication, has this to say about the difficulties of moving ahead:

It's in a company's best interest, and the right thing to do, to look after the professional welfare of its managers. But that never relieves managers of the responsibility to look out for themselves. Managers who deserve promotions may find themselves caught in a bottleneck. Budget restrictions may cause promotions to be deferred, or contraction may limit the number of higher-level positions. It's not your fault, and it's not really the company's fault. But it's *your* career, your life, and your self-satisfaction that are at stake.

It's important to consider your options—consider them seriously. Changing companies, changing careers, or retiring early may be impractical or unnecessarily risky. But I fear these possibilities are never even given a fair hearing by many managers. Try this: instead of asking yourself, "If I got squeezed out of my job, where could I go and what could I do?" ask, "If I were suddenly free to start something new, what else have I always wanted to do with my life?"

The next question is: "How could I get there from here?" What must you add to your present skills and knowledge to start your own business, develop (and possibly patent or publish) a good idea, reduce crime in your community, improve the school system, or start an opera company? What does it take to run for political office, or to teach?

If you are in your career and your organization by choice, of course you want to hang in there. And being passed by for a promotion once isn't the cue to jump ship and start over. But there's room for more than one achievement in your life. Your career should be something you do with your life, not life itself. Your career may stall or run aground, but your life need not founder, nor need it languish like an unfinished book on a bedside table.[1]

[1]Management, *The Levinson Letter,* 15 March, 1982, 1. Reprinted with permission. Copyright The Levinson Institute.

There are many reasons why a career might not advance as quickly as hoped. For example, Amanda Hines's career nearly came to a stop because of her manager's ego. With a background of working in nonprofti institutions, Amanda knew she would have to start low on the corporate totem pole when she decided to transfer her skills to the profit sector. She landed a marketing communications job in an electronics industry corporation in the Boston area, working for a marketing manager whose skills and ego were both considerable, but whose self-confidence was low. Amanda did a good job for two years, though she was unhappy working for a boss who frequently criticized her even for minor things and rarely praised even her most competent work. When a line department in her company offered her a position (unsolicited), she was delighted at the opportunity to more fully utilize her skills and to join a more congenial work environment.

Her boss, however, did not see Amanda's offer as a good opportunity for her, but rather as a setback for himself. He could not refuse to allow her to accept the offer because she had more than fulfilled her initial promise to remain in her first job for at least eighteen months, but he delayed her departure in as many ways as he could. First he neglected to send the personnel material requested of him to the department making the offer. In addition, he secured a promise from her future manager to stay her departure until he could find a replacement; then he procrastinated about filling her position. Her future department was patient at first, but they needed her services as soon as possible. After two months of delay, they informed her that they could afford to wait only two more weeks. Amanda's manager finally relented, under pressure from his human resources manager, but he did so with much acidity, and Amanda took her new job amidst an aura of suspicion created by the fuss and bad-mouthing in which her old boss engaged.

The way to avoid such a situation in your own career is to develop a strategy for advancement: to set yourself some long-range goals and to project some markers along the way to these goals which will tell you whether you are moving closer to the heights you'd like to attain or are just kicking rocks around on the path up. Ask yourself not only what you'd like to have achieved when you retire, but where you think you'd like to be in midcareer, and where you'd have to be to consider yourself a success in ten years, five years, two years. Consider factors of prestige, money, and power; determine how much creativity and originality you'd like to have demonstrated; and above all establish for yourself criteria regarding job satisfaction and job comfort levels. Are you doing what you like to do? Do you like the people with whom you interact? Is the work you are doing having an impact on anything? Do you care? Do you look forward to going to work every day?

If as time progresses, you don't find you are meeting these goals, you should consider a course of action which might include: actively seeking another position, either in or out of your department or company; requesting advancement from your manager; or resigning yourself to a slower pace if you are generally happy with your situation, despite lack of movement. (This latter course, by the way, is not always the least desirable.)

Remember that most business structures are pyramidal. There's more room at the bottom than at the top. Even if you are reasonably good, it's easier to get in than to get ahead; it's easier to get ahead at low levels than at high levels; and it's easier to get ahead than to stay ahead. With every successive move up the corporate or professional ladder, the stakes get higher and the risks become greater. It's often more cost-effective for a company to fire bosses than their underlings, and jobs are sometimes downgraded when vacated to save company money. Therefore, if you've found something you like at a certain level and you can afford to remain at that level financially, your strategy might just be to stay put.

The human resources department at a major Chicago insurance firm illustrates this point. Its staff comprised mainly junior-level human resources professionals—all of whom were highly qualified, many with MBAs or several years of experience. On average, there were three junior people in each of five departments in three divisions. The company wasn't in a growth mode, so the opportunities for advancement were small. However, the group was a very congenial one, and its members respected each other's professionalism and intelligence and liked working together. They produced good work and had fun as a team, and while a few left from time to time to further their careers elsewhere, the majority stayed where they were—for longer than one might expect—because they really enjoyed their work.

If you do wish to move quickly up the corporate hierarchy, there are some things you can do to increase your chances of standing out from the group and making some advancement likely.

Though steady, hard work in a company often yields rewards, there are times when it doesn't. If you find that you are not moving up, despite hard work, one of the things you can do to get ahead is to leave the organization you're with. Changing from one company to another—or from department to department within your company—can often mean a greater increase in salary and title than routine yearly increases offered by most companies, and fast trackers often choose this route. Moreover, job offers from outside will often stimulate an employer to make a counter offer. Remember, though, don't change jobs so often or so quickly that you appear flighty.

When you've been employed in a particular job at a major or well-respected firm for a period of time, you become attractive to competitors and to headhunters whose livelihood depends on finding bright stars to offer corporations. Those who successfully change firms can often earn a 10 percent to 25 percent increase with each move (on top of inflationary increases), while those who work competently in their own departments can usually only count on a 5 percent to 10 percent annual increase, just slightly ahead of inflation. Sometimes, in large corporations in particular, moving from department to department can mean faster promotions, but most companies have limits on wage increases for employees. In fact, they will often pay more to lure outsiders into the company than they will to keep internal employees in the same jobs because they believe the competition is greater outside the corporation than it is within. (You should be aware, however, that most corporations offer benefits other than salary to longtime employees: profit-sharing, for example, or investment opportunities or pension programs. In addition, many companies reward good performers with merit increases, and many companies allow relatively few senior positions to go to outsiders.)

Changing companies can be a successful strategy even if you would really like to spend most of your working life with a particular company. If you aren't moving fast enough, leave for a better job, work at it for a few years, and come back to the original place at a higher level. In most cases, you'll be amazed at how much your stock will rise if you are perceived as being desirable by the competition.

When contemplating a move, especially if your goal is increased money or responsibility, don't undersell yourself. Hold out for what you really want. Chances are if a company really wants you it will come through with the money or the title. In general, avoid lateral moves, unless you are desperate to leave a current situation or you perceive that the job to which you are moving is a step on an excellent career path.

A unique case of twins in similar positions illustrates how important strategy is in getting ahead. Byron and Brian both were armed with Ivy League degrees when they entered the communications department of a major conglomerate headquartered in the Midwest. Both were noted by their manager as go-getters, and both were ambitious. Byron decided the way to get ahead was to move, so after two years, he left his first job and headed East. After twelve years, in his fourth job in his third company, he was head of all of corporate communications at a six-figure salary. His brother stayed with the same corporation for the same period of time and he, too, was promoted at what was a rapid rate for the company. But Brian had to wait until slots became available instead of seeking them out, and each advancement in salary was limited by strict human resources guidelines specifying maximum increases for employees. At the end of the twelve-year period, Brian had risen as far as possible in his company, which was roughly the same size as his brother's. But because the company never felt they had any competition for Brian's services, his salary was not much more than half of his brother's, and his title, too, was lower.

To different degrees, Brian and Byron's careers were both success stories. Arnold Williams, a university classmate of the twins, began a promising career at about the same time in the same field in a Fortune 1000 company in New York. But Arnold made the mistake of making two lateral moves, one in his original company and one to another company, in the first four years of his career. From thence forward, he was perceived as not going anywhere, though his talents and intelligence were probably not much different from the twins', and after the twelve years described above, Arnold was only an assistant vice president at a salary that was roughly half of Brian's and a quarter of Byron's. Thus, how you structure your career—what opportunities you take advantage of and seek out—is an essential ingredient in success.

Be careful if you play this game, however. You must stay in a job long enough to maintain credibility; a resume indicating less than a two-year tenure in most jobs suggests instability, and it is not useful to develop a reputation of leaving departments in the lurch. If you threaten to leave your job for a better position, make sure you really have another job offer. Consider the possibility that there may not be a counteroffer from your boss, that in fact he or she may call your bluff. It is also important to remember not to quit one job until you are sure you have another even if you are unhappy. Not only will you be on the unemployment line if the new job doesn't come through, but you are much less attractive to a potential boss if you are unemployed than if you have a position. Moreover, already being employed when you are hired for a new job gives you bargaining power.

For example, Agnes Burney, right out of college, worked for nearly a year in an administrative position in a publishing house. The job was somewhere between an administrative assistant and an account executive: low-paying, but a good entry-level job nonetheless. Agnes liked the work and for a while looked forward to a career in the publishing world. After ten months she was offered a higher salary at a public relations firm and she accepted the job. It seemed like a good opportunity, and Agnes never considered that the speed with which she was getting ahead could be anything but a plus in her career.

Three months on the new job, however, and she felt she had to get out. PR wasn't her bag. She hated the work, she couldn't keep up with the pace, the people she saw all day long seemed superficial, and the job was not really secure because her client was a difficult one and kept threatening not to renew the agency's contract. When the client finally left the agency, so did Agnes. She wasn't fired, but she had had enough. Living at home, she began beating the pavement. She had had no trouble getting her first two jobs and anticipated none this time; but suddenly she found herself answering insinuating interview questions about why she couldn't stick to a job for more than a few months. She tried to explain the events as best she could, but she could get no corroboration from her past employers. The publishers, who really liked Agnes when she worked there, thought she had been unprofessional to leave so soon; and her second set of managers really hadn't had a chance to evaluate her work. Her record seems to speak for itself. Agnes got out of the situation by returning to graduate school to get an MBA and eventually became a financial analyst; but she was lucky.

Another person who intended to get ahead as fast as he could was Terrence McCloy. He rose through the systems department at a manufacturing company until he secured a fairly senior position. Although the job was a good one, it did not pay a very high salary compared to many line jobs in the company. Terry was impatient to get ahead fast because he had spent several years in the army and several more years traveling before he began his career in systems. He began another job search, not so much with the desire to get another job, but with the hope that by threatening to leave he would force his own employer to raise his salary.

His employer wasn't biting, however, primarily because of centrally mandated salary constraints during a period of slow economic growth, and also because he considered Terry replaceable. He told Terry that if he wanted more salary, he'd have to leave the company. Terry had a family to support and stayed on, but there was a strain between Terry and his boss from then on because the manager was extremely sensitive to what he considered signs of disloyalty to the company. Though Terry had many feelers out, none of them bore results, and he became a joke in the systems department as a perpetual job-seeker. His career virtually stood still after that, and many years later he retired from the company at practically the same level he had achieved before he threatened to leave.

Seeking outside positions means using all your contacts, regardless of whether they are personal friends or professional headhunters. It means acting on inside knowledge about expanding departments or vacant positions, and it means structuring your resume in such a way as to form unique combinations of talents and achievements to fill more and more specialized positions.

In some areas where the job market is tight, stories proliferate about job candidates reading the obituaries to find out what jobs are vacant. While this approach is probably apocryphal, having an inside tip on who's leaving or who's looking can be the edge a job-seeker needs to land a position. For example, Marlene Brueller was sharing a taxi with a fellow worker, going to a meeting in a different part of the city in which they both worked, when the conversation turned to career paths. Though at first neither knew the other was in the job market, their conversation resulted in an exchange of information regarding openings in other institutions in their respective fields. Marlene, a press relations specialist with a commercial bank, called the contact her co-worker had given her, and shortly afterwards landed a better job at another bank, without even looking at a second opportunity. Although chance played an important part in Marlene's rapid transfer, such "chances" can happen frequently if you keep the network open and maintain good communications with others in your field.

Paul Lang's corporate climb went another route. He was tired of his job in a human resources consulting firm. He was an account manager with a lot of customer contact. He wanted a managerial job with less travel and entertaining, in a larger organization. The type of job he wanted wasn't the next obvious step on his career path, and the job locale he sought was in a different type of company than the one in which he worked, so he contacted a headhunter for advice on how to structure his job search. The headhunter, whose specialty was human resources positions, provided enough guidance and contacts for Paul to land a job in a relatively short period of time.

The help Paul received was free, since the headhunter billed the firms seeking people to fill positions, not the candidates themselves. Many people in the business world are often surprised to find headhunters contacting them, even though they are not officially in the job market. Headhunters frequently make it their business to keep as large a stable as possible of available—or potentially available—candidates, and can often be a good starting point in a job search.

Before you make a switch from one job to another, consider your new position carefully. It is very demoralizing to leave one job for another—even if you switched for a variety of good reasons—only to find the problems you left behind duplicated in your new work, or to find a set of new problems worse than the old. Arnold R. Deutsch gives some advice on this score:

CHANGING JOBS—LOOKING DEEP BEFORE YOU LEAP

How does it happen? You find out six months after moving into a new job that the advantages you thought existed have melted away; that you are stuck in a job from which there is no movement but out, that is to start all over again at job finding; that the company is shaky financially, is readying to move to another part of the country, is involved in a merger, or is striking out in a new direction for which your experience does not qualify you.

Obviously, the time to find out about these hazards is *before* you change jobs. Anyone who has ever had a job interview has experienced the probing questions that interviewers ask to find out about *you.* But remarkably few people ever ask more than general, superficial questions about the company; and even these tend to accept what the company person says about it.

Let's look at some questions you should be asking before accepting a new job as well as some possible sources for answers. Here's a checklist of points that will help you build a profile of the company (and could well make a difference in the pattern of your future success or failure on a new job.)

- About the company itself: How long has it been in business? Who are its executives? Is it financially stable? What kind of reputation does it have as an employer?
- What are the company products or services? Is the de-

mand for them growing or diminishing? Sometimes a product or service or a whole industry is in a changing or declining market, with a replacement or a new technique already on the horizon. (Look at the quick growth of word processing or the personal computer.)

- Do the company products face competition from foreign manufacturers that would affect its profits in the U.S.? Plant closings throughout the country underline the importance of this fact.
- Where does the company stand in the industry vis-á-vis its competition? Is it an old prestigious firm or a zesty newcomer? Is it noted for innovation?
- How does it stand on affirmative action? If you're a minority member or a woman, this point could shape your future. Even with today's emphasis on the working woman, there are still firms who do not have an active advancement policy for some employees. A woman hired as a secretary in such a company will probably stay a secretary, no matter how bright or how hard she tries. Carol J. is an example. As assistant in Sales, she talked to clients, handled their orders, and sold the product in the showroom. When it came time for the company's national sales meetings, Carol stayed home (for ten years) until a competitor realized she was a prize sales person and hired her away.
- What does the company offer as benefits? Some companies have more than just basic health insurance; they have stock-buying plans, credit unions, retirement benefits, internal training programs, and tuition for further study. (This could be a big factor in advancement.)
- How does company compensation compare with other firms in the field? What are its policies on raises, overtime, bonuses?
- What is the working environment? Having a pleasant or well-equipped place to work says a lot about the company's regard for its employees, contributes to daily performance, a feeling of well being, and in some cases your health.

HOW YOU CAN FIND OUT WHAT YOU NEED TO KNOW

Unfortunately, the easy sources that come to mind won't help. The company interviewer won't reveal company skeletons, and employment agencies are dedicated to filling the job. But there are other—if less easy—sources open to you:

1. *People who know the company.* These include friends or relatives who have worked there or who know people who have. Maybe they can arrange an introduction to an employee-friend. Social contacts are a good source, too. Fellow club members, or members of your church, may work at the company or know someone who does. However, you have to actively seek out such people and have clear ideas on what to ask them.
2. *Company personnel.* You can meet them at career seminars or open houses. (Watch your newspaper for announcements.) There are company reps at conventions and trade shows that you may meet and talk with. Sometimes, too, companies are involved in community events, which gives you a chance to meet employees informally. Don't, however, depend on a single contact; try to get a cross section of opinion.
3. *Printed material by the company*—the annual report, the company house organ, product brochures, information booklets. Many companies also publish brochures on their history and accomplishments.
4. *Readers' Guide* and other reference sources at the library. Seek out articles that have appeared about the company in business, trade, and professional journals, as well as in national magazines.
5. *Your local paper.* Keep an eye on the business pages for current news.
6. If you have access to a *broker,* get his or her evaluation.
7. *Business reference sources,* such as *Standard & Poor's* and *Dun & Bradstreet,* give useful thumbnail summaries.
8. Study *company ads* in the newspapers, professional magazines in their field, national ads, and on TV.

Before you finish, you may feel like an investigative reporter. But the time will be well spent if it means you move into the right job at the right time.[2]

[2]Deutsch, pp. 137-9.

Another thing you can do to get ahead is to position yourself as the star performer in your group. Impress not only your boss, but your boss's boss, so that when an upper-level position opens up, you're perceived as being ready to fill it. Your boss can't say you're "not seasoned" enough in your job if his or her boss thinks you are. This approach is sometimes trickier than changing companies because you are being judged on real or perceived accomplishments—you really have to be the goods—and you face competition from peers.

Andrea Marino *was* the goods. Without appearing offensively pushy, she managed to fit in quietly and do an excellent job with every project she was assigned. Her specialty was investor relations and she worked for a small firm in New York's Wall Street area which specialized in consulting for several specific types of manufacturing firms. Although shy and modest by nature, she worked efficiently and quickly, and produced quality results. She impressed both clients and superiors with her steady reliability and substantive approach to problems. Moreover, she was as enthusiastic and productive about small projects as large, and she was as willing to labor hard at minor details and production work as she was at more "creative" endeavors. Andrea's talents were both noticed and appreciated, and her rise in the firm was every bit as rapid and spectacular as that of some of her equally talented, but more splashy coworkers who constantly attempted to put themselves in the limelight.

Another strategy for getting ahead, ironic as it may seem, is moving to a parallel or even lower position in a different area for a while, gaining new experience and an additional kind of expertise, then combining your new knowledge and experience with your old in such a way that you become unique and secure a position at a higher level sooner than you would have had you remained on your original career path. Two specialists in organizational behavior, Douglas T. Hall and Lynn Isabella, considered this type of move in a recent article:

> The central issue is whether the individual has chosen the move or had it thrust upon him or her. Some people choose to move down in order to stay in the organization and con-

tinue to use the knowledge and relationships they have built up. Sara, a successful manager, said, "I could have taken a job with another company that would have been a distinct promotion. Yet, I knew I would have to start all over again learning the system. People here know me and know what I can do. That's worth more to me than anything else." Others may choose a move to reduce job stress, to spend more time with their families or to lead a more peaceful existence. As one man remarked, "For the last six years, I had been commuting fifty-five miles to work each way. I had had enough. I wanted to spend more time with my wife and family."

However, in times of retrenchment organizations often need to reduce their staffs. The individual who is forced to move down because of this situation is likely to feel "less well off." Moves necessitated by staff reductions can be especially difficult for persons in the early stages of their careers. They may feel shattered by an organization that they assumed was interested in helping, and may have bitter reactions.

Money is a critical issue in downward moves. Even if a person can adjust to a loss of status and power, reduced income presents a difficult reality. Fortunately, many organizations do not decrease the person's pay (except perhaps when downgrading is due to poor performance). A common way of dealing with pay is to "red circle" the person's salary. The person is kept at the same salary but given no increases until inflation has brought his or her pay into the range of the lower-level position.

A large chemical manufacturing firm uses a special salary category that is outside the regular compensation system. The person's current salary is maintained, and he or she also receives increases. However, the increases are smaller than those the person would have received at the old level and are calculated to reduce the person gradually to the lower pay range. The salary adjustment takes about two years, and, according to the firm's manager of personnel planning, "the person hardly feels the change!"[3]

[3]Lynn Isabella and Douglas T. Hall, "Demotions and Career Growth," *Training and Development Journal* 38, no. 4 (1984): 62–4. Copyright 1984. American Society for Training and Development. Reprinted with permission. All rights reserved.

In fact, many corporations encourage the development of broad-based experience in their managers by building a series of major moves into a promising employee's career path. Line people may receive a temporary assignment in a staff area (and vice versa) to handle a specal project, or may even be routinely assigned a variety of tours in areas they may never have thought of. And many a staff member working on a project with a line manager has developed an interest in the manager's work and impressed the manager with his or her own skills, and moved permanently into the client department. Generally, a corporation's senior management welcomes such changes as they bring fresh approaches to old problems and keep morale high by providing a variety of advancement opportunities for employees.

One of the most important things you can do to ensure success is to be self-aware. Know when you're getting stale and when it's time to move on. Know whether your ability to make yourself essential is strong. Assess your own ideas: are they fresh? Do they improve on the existing patterns in your business? Are you pitching your efforts in support of the bottom line?

Stay on top of what's happening. Is the economy OK? Is your industry? Your company? How's your boss doing? Your department? Your boss's boss? Is your function thought to be important in your company or industry? On a personal level, are the vital signs toward you changing? Are you seen as a star or a dog? Are your assignments and projects as crucial as they ever were, or are they diminishing in importance?

Some people are more self-aware than others about their careers, and prosper more because of this. Karen Montgomery, for example, was going strong as a campus recruiter for a West Coast commercial bank. She was full of novel ideas that worked, and her energy and innovativeness made her a favorite both in the office and on campus. Her site visits usually netted the company more applications than those of any of her colleagues. But after four years of college relations work, her techniques became stale. She ceased to sense the changing moods on college campuses and did not change her tactics accordingly. Luckily, she was perceptive enough to be aware of her diminishing effectiveness and suggest to her boss that she transfer to another position where she could get a fresh start. Because she had an excellent track record, she was moved up into a management position where she coordinated the activities of the other campus recruiters, and thus her career did not really suffer.

Marcus Williams, on the other hand, did not notice that he was losing freshness in his job as a writer for a meat processing company's internal newspaper in Chicago. Once able to report interesting news in a readable fashion, his prose became more and more wooden as he settled into his job and lost the sense of excitement that comes with a new challenge. Unfortunately, while his senior editor recognized Marcus's shortcomings, Marcus himself didn't. He insisted his prose was read as widely as ever, and was insisting on the same thing while waiting on the unemployment line. Unable to adjust to a changing environment, Marcus was asked to resign.

In a different instance, Eric Palmer made the mistake of not looking at the whole picture. He worked in a human resources subdepartment that specialized in running the corporation's suggestion system. His task was to assess the need for and the feasibility of the suggestions submitted by employees. He worked diligently—even feverishly—interviewing people, writing memos and proposals, and publishing reports on the suggestions submitted. His work—voluminous as it was—was highly appreciated by his boss, whose personal style was to generate as much noise and confusion around a project as possible before coming out with a solution. Eric knew his boss liked to look busy, and he fell right in with his boss's style.

What Eric didn't pick up, however, was that his boss was losing credibility with the rest of his colleagues in his department and around the corporation. People were conscious of the lack of real value of the output Eric's boss was generating. And Eric was seen as a pale version of his manager. So when Eric's boss lost his position, the subdepartment was "reorganized," and Eric lost his job as well. The situation came as a complete surprise to Eric, who simply did not think about the position of his manager in the department. While it may be argued that Eric's fate was inevitable, other employees of an incompetent supervisor have escaped their boss's fate by demonstrating some signs of independence and by establishing allies other than their immediate superior.

Another case of a fallen star came when Pamela Bujones erred one day in filling out an expense form for an administrative department in the company for which she worked. Her job required attention to a great many details, and Pam was viewed by her boss and others in the department as dependable and good at her job. She had been promoted several times to a position with a fair degree of authority, but, unfortunately, she had become conceited and complacent about her position in the department. One afternoon, through sheer carelessness, she made an error that caused a $16,000 problem. A bit of the care she used to lavish on her responsibilities could have prevented the mistake. Because of her past accomplishments, she did not lose her job, but the incident shook up some of her superiors and they subtly began overseeing her work and giving her less and less responsibility. Even though the carelessness never recurred, the damage had been done. Pam never received another promotion.

In trying to make a success of your own career, it is important to keep all of the above considerations in mind. But, most of all, it is important to keep faith with yourself. Maintain your belief in your own abilities. Be confident, assertive, aggressive. A story overheard in the elevator of a major New York City commercial bank illustrates the fact that compliance isn't equated with cooperativeness: The manager of a vital area kept a job candidate waiting an hour for an interview. When she finally called the candidate in, she said, "Your resume looks very strong, but I can't hire anyone for this position who has so little self-respect that he can be kept waiting an hour for an appointment. This job requires aggressiveness, and your behavior indicates that you just don't have it."

Chapter 9
When You Become
a Manager

The goal of many an employee is to become a manager. The high point of many an employee's career is becoming a manager. Also, the downfall of many of an employee is becoming a manager.

Though management status is frequently seen as and used as a reward for good work, efficient and talented employees often do not realize that being a boss requires a completely different set of talents and strengths than doing a good job on a project or pleasing a client. Though an individual may have succeeded in performing tasks and accomplishing projects, he or she may fall apart when faced with management decisions.

The two most essential management traits are people skills and organizational abilities. However, a person who gets along well with colleagues or clients cannot always maintain good relationships with subordinates; and a person who can organize and juggle the many facets of a client relationship or a major project can collapse when asked to manage an entire department consisting of many people and projects and relationships, all at various stages of development.

Moreover, first management-level jobs frequently come with an additional source of frustration: the low-level or middle-level manager may be in charge of implementing someone else's (his or hers own manager's) ideas, and he or she may not always agree with these ideas.

When you are fortunate enough to become a manager—and becoming one *is* a good opportunity—bear in mind the following pitfalls, and try to avoid them whenever possible:

PEOPLE PROBLEMS

We have already discussed ways of getting along with colleagues and bosses. Management brings with it the additional necessity to get along with subordinates—secretaries, administrative assistants, and professionals who report to you. And "getting along with" has a host of connotations above and beyond being perceived as a "nice guy." Managing people is considerably tougher and more emotionally draining for most people than managing projects.

The most common error new managers make is trying to maintain the reputation established in premanagement days of being "one of the team," "a real friend," "someone you can always talk to and count on," "someone who is fun to be with." As a new manager, you will suddenly realize that not all of the decisions you have to make are going to please people, and that these tough decisions are ones you are going to make anyway. For some people, the first experience of making an unpopular decision—not wrong, just unpopular—can be devastating. All at once you are transmogified from "one of the gang" to "the boss." Instead of joining the others in the time-honored activity of complaining about the boss, you are now the object of complaints by others. It takes a tough hide to make this transition.

Elaine Carter, for example, thought everything was going beautifully when she was promoted from communications consultant in a large commercial bank to manager of the department of which she had previously been a part. She had done an excellent job on the projects to which she had been assigned, had the most seniority of all the consultants, was universally liked and respected, and was chronologically the oldest of the consultants. When her boss retired, Elaine and the senior managers in the department considered her promotion a logical step. What Elaine did not realize, however, was that the expectations of some of her colleagues were unrealistically inflated, and her appointment to the job engendered jealousy among these former peers.

Her naively enthusiastic first decisions—about what projects to accept for the department and to whom to assign them— were met with resistance and even thinly veiled hostility. She detected coldness on the part of some of her former colleagues, and in one case encountered refusal to undertake a task on the grounds that the employee was too busy. The signs of insubordination bothered Elaine for two reasons: she thought these people were her friends and would gladly cooperate with her in her success, and she worried that because of this resistance she would not be able to do the job she was selected to do.

Fortunately for Elaine, her own manager was as perceptive as she was about the trouble brewing, and had had extensive experience in dealing with such situations. He also had confidence in Elaine and wanted her to succeed, for both her own sake and the sake of the department as a whole. With her full knowledge, he defused the situation by transferring two of the most outwardly resistant of Elaine's subordinates (neither of whom were incompetent and both of whom had long records of success on projects) to other areas of the department. He staged these transfers as part of a general reorganization, which included Elaine's promotion as well, so that the other employees who reported to Elaine would not perceive these moves as capitulation to insubordination.

Elaine's own even temper and steady good work helped as well, and before too long, the situation stabilized, with Elaine firmly in control of the department. The other members of it maintained their respect for her, though the friendship she had had with them previously cooled permanently. Elaine accepted her new role as boss, not colleague.

Mitchell Waterman encountered a situation very similar to Elaine's in a company dedicated to manufacturing computer software. But where Elaine accepted the growing personal distance between herself and her former peers, Mitchell had an emotional need to be "one of the gang." His promotion to manager of his department, accompanied by the same kind of jealousy and resentment Elaine detected, rankled him and he reacted by increasing his attempts to stay in his employee's good graces at all costs. He increased his invitations to them for drinks, for squash games, for seeing movies, and for lunch dates, being as open and forthright as possible on all issues—even management issues. The result was that though the jealousy did not decrease, the respect Mitchell's former colleagues had for him did. They began to see his appeal to their friendship as a weakness, and they used this need to get their own way on issues and projects. Mitchell was afraid to cross anyone or say "no" for fear of losing their support or damaging his reputation as one of the guys, and the output of the department grew slimmer and slimmer.

Mitchell did not regain the friendship of those in his department, and he lost their support as well. Despite warnings from his own manager, Mitchell could not face the loss of his former "friends" and could not make the department work; he was finally relieved of his managerial responsibilities.

Although it sometimes hurts to take the reins, your success as a manager depends on doing so with authority. It is important to maintain your position or opinion if you think it is right, and although you should explain your ideas to your subordinates and listen to their differences and grievances, you should not be swayed by public opinion alone. If you give in when you do not want to, you invite a host of problems more difficult to contend with than lack of popularity. You will be seen as indecisive, a waverer who does not have the courage of his or her convictions, not smart enough to think through a problem and arrive at a conclusion you can live with, and someone who can easily be pushed around. Your credibility will suffer and your management tenure may be limited.

Conversely, you have to remember not to establish your authority with too much arrogance. Firmness and humility make a more acceptable combination for most subordinates to accept than blind authority combined with impatience.

For instance, one manager, Teddy Kolodyne, who was promoted to the head of a professional recruiting unit in a major corporation, bounded into the top slot full of good ideas—and not willing to listen to any competing "good" ideas. He was widely respected for his innovativeness and for his former success in hiring for his firm, and many of the ideas he brought to the company were now widely accepted as "policy." But his were not the only ideas that had made his department a success in the past, and his ego was not able to share the spotlight. He antagonized many of his former colleagues—also successes in their own right—by rejecting without consideration any ideas that did not originate with himself, and before long more than half his department had either transferred or left the company. The worse Teddy's interpersonal relations became, the more obstinate he became; and finally, with virtually no productive subordinates, he, himself, was asked to leave the company.

The lesson is, make your decisions, but listen to opposing views; consider them; accept them when practical; and if you are rejecting them, explain why. Treat people as intelligent beings, and remember that it takes more than a captain to make a team.

Perhaps the most disturbing activity you as a manager will have to undertake is firing someone. Although such a job is frequently upsetting and even heart-rending, there are times when it is unavoidable and for the best—either for the company, the department, the client, or for the dismissed employee. Most people who avoid the decision to fire discover that the situation only deteriorates if postponed.

For example, Mortimer Berkeley was a good manager in general—friendly but firm, innovative yet open to the ideas of others, independent yet fatherly to those in his employ. He ran a good shop in a marketing firm, and rarely had to fire anyone. The one or two misfits he or others had hired had discovered for themselves that they and the department were not a good match, and they had found other jobs.

Then he made the mistake of accepting for employment an older man—four years from retirement—from another department. The man convinced him that his lack of success in his old department was due to a unique personality clash between himself and his former boss. Mortimer thought he was hiring an experienced, productive, easy-to-work-with individual, but what he really hired was a superb actor. The man was incompetent, lazy, and contentious. Because of the man's age and because Mortimer knew the man had financial pressures, Mortimer was reluctant to see any signs of poor performance. He overlooked serious lapses, and kept up a fiction that the man was simply "adjusting slowly" to his new responsibilities. Before long, the man had lost two of the department's best clients, and had sowed the seeds of dissension among the other professionals, who saw their own efforts undermined by the man's incompetence.

By the time Mortimer faced reality and decided he had to do something, he had, unfortunately, written several performance reviews that had not reflected the man's problems. He began to take official note of the problems, but another year went by before Mortimer had enough incidents recorded and documented to make a case for firing the man. And, to make matters worse, the man was then only one and a half years from retirement and the senior management of the firm decided to wait the last eighteen months and let him retire. Thus, though Mortimer's department was not unalterably ruined, his reluctance to fire someone resulted in four years' worth of diminished performance.

If you have to fire someone, do so after thorough consideration, after discussion about the problems with the employee, and after complete documentation of the person's failings. No employee should be surprised by being fired. Do so in private, with discretion, and with support—even to the extent of helping the employee find another job. In most cases, the individual who is let go is—at one level—glad to be out of a bad situation, despite the money pressures that losing a job entails.

Hiring presents a different set of problems for a manager. There are several important points to bear in mind when hiring an employee, whether expanding your staff or replacing a staff member. First, do some strategic planning to determine whether the slot you want to fill is really necessary to your organization, and whether the parameters of the job are going to remain the same in the foreseeable future. Make sure you know exactly what responsibilities the person will have, and select a person whose qualifications meet your needs. If the job or the department's responsibilities are going to change, be sure the new person will be able to meet the new requirements. If you see staff cutbacks in the near future, hold up on filling a vacant slot. It is far easier to not fill a spot than it is to fire an employee.

Next, if possible, let a human resources recruiting expert in your company or in a recruiting firm do the initial screening for you, especially if you are hiring from outside and not considering internal transfers. If you present some of the broad requirements for the job to a recruiter, you can save yourself a lot of time. Often there are dozens of applicants for a single spot; you do not want to see them all. Moreover, most employers are not as adept at the interviewing process as trained and experienced recruiters. Once a recruiter has compiled a manageable list of reasonable candidates, you and other key people in your organization (especially those who will be interacting with the new employee) should speak with the applicants. Try to see the candidates in various settings: let someone take the strongest candidates to lunch; let another person talk to the person in a formal setting, in a conference room, perhaps; two other people should meet the candidate together to see how he or she responds in a situation other than one-on-one. If a candidate is at ease in various circumstances, he or she probably feels pretty comfortable with the organization. It is very important that you (and others in your department) not only feel a candidate is qualified for a position, but that you feel comfortable with the person and like him or her. If there are traits about the person you do not like or trust, you can be sure that such characteristics will become magnified—often dangerously so— after the person is on board.

Be certain to explain to a candidate the responsibilities, challenges, and problems that the job will entail. Also, point out any areas that are unknowns. Then try to ascertain from the candidate what kind of experience and capabilities he or she has that will enable him or her to do the job you require. Concrete evidence—written reports or articles, completed projects, etc.—should be produced whenever possible to establish the candidate's credentials. Ask probing questions to determine the expertise of the candidate in areas in which he or she claims to be proficient. The candidate should be able to talk in-depth about areas on which he or she has worked.

It is also important to check a candidate's references. If you know someone who knows the candidate, contact that person and ask frankly about the person's work record and interpersonal skills. (Be sure, however, that you do not place a candidate in an awkward position with his or her present employer who might not know that the person is looking for another job.) If you do not know a candidate's references, do not rely soley on their letters of reference. Call the references directly. People will rarely put anything negative in writing, but they might be willing to give you a straight story over the telephone.

As a final part of the selection process, if possible, give the person a trial run at the job. Devise a test—a writing sample, a free-lance miniproject, etc.—which will provide you with a real piece of work to judge. (Make it clear to the candidate whether you intend to pay for this service or not. Candidates have been known to bill potential employers for "free-lance" charges incurred durng the interview process. Put this agreement in writing.)

Once a new hire is on board, make sure that either you or someone else on your staff is prepared to give that person the time and attention he or she needs to learn the ropes and understand the new responsibilities. Many new employees who only last a few months are the victims of a "sink or swim" attitude on the part of employers.

To be a successful people manager, you must maintain a balanced approach to your staff and your superiors. It takes both flexibility and ingenuity to keep your boss happy by implementing his or her ideas; to keep the professionals on your staff happy by establishing meaningful responsibilities and standards; and to keep your secretary busy, but not overworked, and faithful, but not beaten down.

Be consistent and even-tempered in your approach to people. A manager who flies off the handle regularly or says one thing on Monday and another on Tuesday soon either becomes the butt of many office jokes and loses credibility, or makes his or her employees so nervous that they cannot perform efficiently. Listen to your staff's suggestions, gripes, and requests; admit when you don't know something, and don't feel you always have to have the last word; don't let personal problems interfere with your consistently patient treatment of your staff; and keep yourself accessible and respond promptly; don't be the cause of your department's missing a deadline.

Margaret Whalen failed miserably at managing because she found it difficult to take the above advice, given her by a human resources expert when she first was asked to head a team of communications professionals. She unnerved her staff by frequently changing her attitude towards them. When she was in a happy mood, she treated them jovially; when things were going wrong at home, she barked and complained at work. She undermined the professionalism of her own operation by assigning a "rush" project to a staff member one day, then insisting that a "high priority rush" project be done before the "rush" project the next day. She found it difficult to remember what everyone was doing, and she really didn't get along on a personal level with those around her.

The human resources department began to worry about Margaret's shop when a succession of secretaries stayed only an average of five weeks, and when four out of five professionals on her staff asked for transfers within three months—all with the same reason: managerial incompetence. No amount of advice or counseling seemed to work in this case, and Margaret was finally asked to leave.

ORGANIZATIONAL PROBLEMS

Interaction with people represents only half the responsibility a new manager must assume; keeping up with the work load represents another. Quite often, the amount of work or number of projects given to a department or area head is staggering. It often seems as though those up the line a bit have no concept of how much work an individual or group can handle. Sometimes it seems as though there is enough work for twice the number of people a department includes. The reverse can also be true. A new manager often finds him- or herself with a staff of several and projects enough for only one or two.

If you are faced with the former situation, you should—very early in the game—take accurate stock of what your department is being asked to do. Know what your people are capable of producing—and producing well, to your credit and their own—and how much work they are being asked to do. If there is a large discrepancy, make a recommendation for more staff (or minimally for some free-lance help during periods of overload), or draw up priorities and notify your own manager at once if lower priority items cannot be done. Never get yourself into the position of taking on more than you or your group can deliver. The sooner you take a stand on this issue, the easier it will be in the long run. Even if you are not given extra staff, those giving your department the work will know you are understaffed and cannot possibly do everything they are asking.

To illustrate: Marcella Connors came to a new managerial job in the systems area of a large insurance concern fresh from a similar position in a data processing firm. In her old job, the work she and her department did was the bread and butter of the company. There were many departments like hers and the business's upper echelon were keenly aware of the capabilities and limitations of departments assigned certain projects. They also knew how much time and effort each project would take. The senior officers of Marcella's new company were more worried about their clients than about the computer support required for their accounts, and were not realistic about what a data processing support group could do. Marcella, luckily, recognized this discrepancy immediately and made priorities and limitations the first subject she discussed with her new boss. Before she allowed herself to fail to do all she was assigned, she spelled out what she saw as looming productivity problems. The end result—achieved fairly soon—was a sharply increased staff. With a larger staff, Marcella achieved what her boss wanted to, and no problems ensued.

Barry Dessiner faced a similar problem when he took over an administrative support function in a major accounting firm. His previous experience, however, was not as directly related to his new position as was Marcella's, and Barry was not able to predict the kinds of problems he would have. He assumed his staff would receive a realistic amount of work and would be able to handle it. It was a full four months before he understood that the volume was terrific, and that he and his staff couldn't manage the work even staying an additional three to four hours daily. Moreoever, morale was low because his subordinates worked long hours without extra pay and still were perceived as not fulfilling their responsibilities. It took Barry many months of negotiation with his superiors, and several staff resignations, to get the situation under control. His staff was finally increased, but so were hard feelings, and Barry's position in the corporation remained tenuous for several years as a result.

The reverse situation can also be a problem. Manny Kaufmann took over a human resources professional recruitment area in an established firm. The firm was so well established, as a matter of fact, that there was really very little for Manny and his staff of seven to do. After several weeks of waiting in vain for the big work load to be placed on his desk, Manny decided to take some initiative. Even though his own managers seemed content to leave Manny alone and for some reason thought he was doing a very good job, he did not want to risk suddenly being called to task for producing nothing. He drew up a plan—virtually his own job description—involving strategic manpower planning, recruitment, internal training, and comparative industry studies; he proceeded to initiate some thinking on the part of his senior management; and he began to develop a proactive department that would become a model for the industry.

It is important to keep an accurate overview of your department's workload. It is also important to keep track of each individual project being done in your department. This does not mean you should not delegate work. You should do so, but you should also be sure the people in charge of each project keep you informed as to progress. Moreover, the information you receive should not be limited to positive achievements. You should receive word of problems as soon as they occur. Be sure you are told not only about projects completed, but about projects during their various stages of development, and about projects held up or not completed.

Kingman Jerrold took over a publications department with a senior editor of long tenure in the company reporting to him. The editor was used to working very independently, and persistently ignored Kingman's requests to show him all copy at all stages of development and to keep him abreast of any problems. What he received from the editor was a rosy picture of how well everything was going; it was not until issues of several publications were delayed for various reasons that he realized he was not getting the whole story. It became a constant battle for information between Kingman and the editor, and at times it looked like the editor would win. The editor was not really incapable, so there were no strong grounds for firing him, especially since he had fifteen years of service to the organization and was over fifty-eight. Kingman's only break came when the editor decided on early retirement because of the "pressure" Kingman was subjecting him to. Kingman then was able to hire a more responsive editor.

STRATEGIES FOR MANAGEMENT SUCCESS

Overcoming people problems and organizational difficulties is not the whole secret to management success. You should develop strategies to enable you to pursue your goals. In the first place, maintain a firm sense of direction. Know what your management objectives are. Set yourself business goals, and don't waver in striving to attain them. This doesn't mean that you should be inflexible; you should always consider alternatives to your way of doing things. It does mean, however, that you should not be sidetracked in working toward your objectives. Peter Drucker suggests,

> A manager's job should be based on a task that has to be done to attain the company's objectives. It should always be a real job—one that makes a visible and, if possible, measurable contribution to the success of the enterprise. It should have the broadest range rather than the narrowest scope and authority. The manager should be directed and controlled by the objectives of performance rather than by his boss.[1]

Pursue your goals in an organized, logical way. In trying to keep much in your head at once, try as well to keep your cool. If

[1]Peter F. Drucker, *The Effective Executive* (New York: Harper & Row, 1967), p. 52.

you are well-organized and a good planner, if you can delegate well and know how and when to set priorities, and if you are realistic about the time it takes to do a project well, you will find these skills advantageous in becoming an effective manager.

Another important ingredient in developing your managerial skills is maintaining contacts with your managerial peers, and maintaining interest in your work. Keeping up with others—what they are doing at work, how they are advancing professionally, what work-related courses or programs they are attending— helps you keep your own activities in perspective. Keeping up with the latest trends in your industry or line of work is also important for a manager, since good management means knowing what the competition is doing and what the state of the art is, and trying to be one step ahead of the rest in being innovative and imaginative in doing your business. Staying up-to-date, taking courses, reading books and articles on both your business area and management topics can do a lot to help you keep the enthusiasm and innovativeness that probably helped you get the management job in the first place.

Knowing which of your skills and activities are the most important to your success is also important. A recent article in the human resources development publication *Training* presents a list of critical managerial competencies (see Figure 9.1).

Another perspective on this issue is expressed by Peter Drucker. He believes that a manager should ask him or herself what he or she can contribute to an organization:

> The effective executive focuses on contribution. He looks up from his work and outward toward goals. He asks: "What can I contribute that will significantly affect the performance and the results of the institution I serve?" His stress is on responsibility.
>
> The focus on contribution is the key to effectiveness: in a man's own work—its content, its level, its standards, and its impacts; in his relations with others—his superiors, his associates, his subordinates; in his use of the tools of the executive such as meetings or reports.
>
> The great majority of executives tend to focus downward. They are occupied with efforts rather than with results. They worry over what the organization and their superiors "owe" them and should do for them. And they are conscious above

Importance rating	Survey rank & competency
Super critical	1. Listen actively 2. Give clear, effective instructions 3. Accept your share of responsibility for problems 4. Identify real problem
Highly critical	5. Manage time; set priorities 6. Give recognition for excellent performance 7. Communicate decisions to employees 8. Communicate effectively (orally) 9. Shift priorities if necessary 10. Explain work 11. Obtain and provide feedback in two-way communication sessions
Critical	12. Write effectively 13. Prepare action plan 14. Define job qualifications 15. Effectively implement organizational change 16. Explain and use cost reduction methods 17. Prepare and operate within a budget 18. Develop written goals 19. Justify new personnel and capital equipment 20. Participate in seminars and read

FIGURE 9.1   Twenty Critical Managerial Competencies

all of the authority they "should have." As a result, they render themselves ineffectual.

The head of one of the large management consulting firms always starts an assignment with a new client by spending a few days visiting the senior executives of the client organization one by one. After he has chatted with them about the assignment and the client organization, its history and its people, he asks (though rarely, of course, in these words): "And what do *you* do that justifies your being on the payroll?" The great majority, he reports, answer: "I run the accounting department," or "I am in charge of the sales force." Indeed, not uncommonly, the answer is, "I have 850 people working under me." Only a few say, "It's my job to give our managers the information they need to make the right decisions," or "I am responsible for finding out what products the customer will want tomorrow," or "I have to think through and prepare the decisions the president will have to face tomorrow."

The man who focuses on efforts and who stresses his downward authority is a subordinate no matter how exalted his title and rank. But the man who focuses on contribution and who takes responsibility for results, no matter how junior is in the most literal sense of the phrase, "top management." He holds himself accountable for the performance of the whole.[2]

Some people are not designed for management at all, and if you are one of these individuals, set your sights on rising through the ranks as an expert project person and steer away from management. The challenges are different, and so are the rewards. Many people do not enjoy management and find greater satisfaction in accomplishing with distinction the basic work their departments do. Many corporations know this management/star-performer differential exists and encourage non-management types to excel in individual work.

If you are anxious about taking a management job, test yourself in the way Mary Miles suggests in an article called "The Trauma of Promotion" in *Computer Decisions* magazine:

BEFORE AND AFTER

Promotion anxiety can be classified by two basic stages: *before* the actual job change, when you have to decide whether or not you should accept; and *after* the promotion, when you're nervously surveying your new domain.

Before. . .

If you're smart, this is the time to do some serious soul-searching. "Some people are so concerned with the gratification of a promotion and the additional salary that they don't spend enough time thinking about whether they are suited for the additional responsibilities," observes Loren Belker in *The First-Time Manager.* Here are some factors to consider during such an analysis:

[2]Drucker, *The Effective Executive,* pp. 52–3.

- Do you understand the company's operations and overall objectives? Can you identify with them easily and are they in harmony with your own ultimate goals?
- Will you get the help and support you need, especially in the difficult adjustment period? Rosalind Forbes, president of Forbes Associates, a New York consultancy specializing in stress management, says people should realize that "in about the fourth to sixth month, there may be a letdown, which is a normal aftermath of change. During this time, a lot of self-questioning will take place. After having worked extra hard to prove you can do the job, you'll probably start asking yourself if this is what you really wanted—if it's all worth it." If you have good rapport with your superiors, it can turn into "positive stress."
- Are you prepared to devote extra time and energy to stay abreast of your job and your field? Help from the top brass is essential, but you must also be willing to seek out education, training, and knowledge.
- Are you ready to develop a managerial outlook and approach? Ascending the career ladder implies a different mindset. This means you must keep some distance between you and your former peers—particularly if they will now be your subordinates. This can be difficult, alienating—even painful—and the way you handle it will greatly affect your credibility as a new boss.
- Are you willing to risk the inevitable mistakes and failures that go hand in hand with learning something new? Are you mature enough to learn from those mistakes, rather than allow them to make you defensive or insecure?
- Can you delegate responsibilities? Patti McVay, president of Fifth Season Travel (Indianapolis), has increased her agency's growth by an astounding ten thousand percent since she took over in 1977. She believes that when people are promoted they often feel they must do everything. In some cases, they hold onto the old responsibilities for dear life, and try to field all the new ones at the same time. During the meteoric rise of Fifth Season, McVay has had to change her management style dramatically, relinquishing certain responsibilities she once feared losing in order to build an effective middle management.
- Do you understand the politics and power relationships that operate within your company and your department?
- Can you get along with a wide variety of people? If you're

a loner and the proposed job requires a high level of interaction with superiors and subordinates, you could run into trouble. Constant cultivation of interpersonal and communication skills is necessary for most managerial positions; these skills are inextricably linked to managerial success.

. . .And after

You've accepted the promotion, and several months later you're still fretting about whether or not you made the right decision. You worked so hard to get here—and now you find you have to work even harder to prove yourself all over again. It's a never-ending process, especially if you're already gearing yourself up for the *next* promotion. Here are some guidelines for settling into the new job with a minimum of trauma for you, your subordinates, and the company:

- Take care of yourself by relaxing and exercising regularly. Don't neglect your physical or mental health. You're probably under more mental and physical stress than ever before.
- Don't be too eager to institute sweeping changes. "Many new young leaders make their lives more difficult by assuming they have to use all their new-found power immediately," according to Belker in *The First-Time Manager.* "The key word is restraint. . . . You're the one who's on trial with your subordinates, not they with you."
- Make sure you develop good communication patterns with subordinates, as well as superiors. "Your subordinates will have more to say about your future than your superiors," says Belker. Remember, you'll ultimately be judged by how effectively your group performs.
- After you've been in the position for several weeks, Belker suggests you have a formal meeting with each of your subordinates. Your job in these sessions is to listen brilliantly.
- You will most likely run up against an employee or two who prefers the previous boss. Just remember you can't win over everyone. Good communications, objectivity, and patience will stand you in good stead and if you're a good manager, even the reluctant ones will come around.

- Make sure you follow the rules you set for your subordinates. A "do as I say, not as I do" attitude is sure to weaken your position with subordinates.
- Be prepared to pay attention to employee needs, even if it involves going to bat for them with your superiors. Your genuine concern will help establish a valuable team spirit.
- Transmit your loyalty on corporate goals, policies, and decisions to your workers. If you find this to be a difficult task, you're probably working for the wrong company.
- Work at grooming your own replacement. Patti McVay believes that "the more important you make someone else, the more important *you'll* be." People have lost out on promotions because they haven't spent enough effort preparing someone to take their place. Even if the person who becomes your "understudy" is promoted out from under you, says Loren Belker, you'll be "establishing a reputation of being an outstanding developer of people, which will add to your own promotability."
- Have the courage to admit when you've made a mistake or gotten in over your head, and don't be afraid to ask for help. If, however, your company is intolerant of mistakes, ask yourself if you're in the right place.
- You can't manufacture self-confidence out of thin air, but it often helps to *act* as if you are a secure and capable leader. The way you speak, hold and move your body, your expression, the way you dress all carry messages to those around you.[3]

If, after all your consideration, you are one of those who chooses a management track, you will find that your choice can be both interesting and rewarding.

[3]Reprinted from *Computer Decisions,* July 1984, pp. 88–102. Copyright 1984, Hayden Publishing Company.

Chapter 10
Those Who Fail

Those who don't *seem* as though they're "making it" in the corporate world often aren't. Although they might appear to be fixtures for a while—and sometimes forever—doing things that brighter lights are too busy to handle, or mopping up routine details after the imaginative, conceptual work is done by others, they are often the first ones cut when budget reductions come round. Years ago, staff areas were known as havens for dead wood; today, with service positions requiring more and more specialized knowledge, most staff areas will not tolerate those who aren't productive any more than line areas will.

This is not to say that all errors or misjudgments represent complete failure. Peters and Waterman, in *In Search of Excellence,* explain that successful organizations have to try many new ideas in order to make progress, and that some of these ideas must, of course, fail. They say,

> A special attribute of the success-oriented, positive, and innovating environment is a substantial tolerance for failure. James Burke, J & J's CEO, says one of J & J's tenets is that "you've got to be willing to fail." He adds that General Johnson, J & J's founder, said to him, "If I wasn't making mistakes, I wasn't making decisions." Emerson's Charles Knight argues: "You need the ability to fail. You cannot innovate unless you are willing to accept mistakes." Tolerance for failure is a very specific part of the excellent company culture—and that lesson comes directly from the top.

Champions have to make lots of tries and consequently suffer some failures or the organization won't learn.[1]

What we are speaking about is the kind of failure that cannot be classified as trial and error; that is debilitating and demoralizing to an organization. It is the kind of failure that is recurring and hampers productivity.

Some people appear to meet with repeated failure in the business world. They can't seem to hold any job for more than a year and a half, despite what look like good qualifications; they send out hundreds of letters of application and never elicit any responses; they attend every self-help course available to job-seekers without being able to assimilate any of the information provided; and they frequently seem to have corresponding problems in their personal relations as well. In general, people who can't hold onto jobs lose them because they are uncooperative, incompetent, or both. People who can't land jobs appear—and usually are—unfocused, insincere about wanting a job, or misguided about the match between their skills and those required for the position they are seeking. Such people are sometimes obnoxious as well, and though most employers who have fired employees say they have done so because of nonproductivity, if an employee has been unpleasant, it probably didn't help the situation.

If you fear that you are a repeated loser—either because you are removed from jobs frequently or do not find jobs in the first place—try to sit back and do some more self-assessment. Even if there seem to be specific, logical reasons for each individual failure, if you feel you are suffering an extreme number of rejections and establishing a pattern of failure, do something about it. First, try to determine what it is you are doing that others are not responding to in a positive way. Then try to become more conscious of the ramifications of what you are doing. And finally, the hardest step, try to change.

[1]Thomas J. Peters & Robert H. Waterman, Jr., *In Search of Excellence* (New York: Harper & Row, 1982), p. 223.

TYPES OF LOSERS

THE INCOMPETENT

This is the most common type of loser in the business world: the person who simply has no idea of how to finish a job or take responsibility for his or her project or actions. The incompetent cannot meet deadlines, cannot produce acceptable work, and cannot convince people of his or her ability to stay on top of a situation. Sometimes this person has landed a job over his or her head, or the job description changed over a period of time and he or she has not upgraded his or her skill base accordingly. Sometimes the person has failed at an initial job and, because he or she was a nice person, was reassigned to another area in which he or she had no skill base whatsoever. At other times, the person really is competent, but appears flighty or silly, or immature and unable to assume responsibility. If you recognize a hint of the incompetent in yourself, your best move is to reassess your strengths and determine whether you are in the right position for you. It is no shame to select to pursue a career based on individual projects, for instance, if people management is not something you can handle; or to opt for a career path in which you use your technical knowledge instead of attempting analysis or synthesis if these are not your strengths; or to settle into a writing job and not pursue the next step, which might be an editing job. Sometimes moving up a career path really involves acquiring or perfecting new skills, and not everyone is capable of or wants to do this. Be honest with yourself. It is better to succeed at one level than to fail at a "higher" level.

THE JACK-OF-ALL-TRADES

This person typically tries to do everyone else's job in addition to his own. While he may be a basically competent person, the jack-of-all-trades can't keep his fingers out of any pie. He can't delegate authority, so he does his subordinates' jobs as well as his own; he can't share, so he usurps or volunteers for his peers' jobs in addition to his own; and he can't respect authority, so he tries to do his boss's job without being asked. He fails because he cannot possibly do his job well with all the other commitments he has undertaken, and because he has spread himself too thin. This type of person also frequently applies for various other positions in his department, not always because it represents a move up the corporate ladder, but simply because he thinks he can do the job. The jack-of-all-trades is commonly motivated by a desire to prove himself and earn praise. What he is really crying to the world is, "See how clever I am and how much I can do." He might also be saying, "I can do it better than anyone else." Clearly, if you know you have a tendency to overextend your job into other people's purviews, your next step is to identify the parameters of your own position and stay within them. Ask your boss for help in doing this if you cannot do it yourself. You will be more productive all around if you do not spread yourself too thin, and chances are you will antagonize fewer of your fellow workers.

THE PROMISER

Another example of a person biting off more than he can chew is the promiser. The promiser says "yes" to every assignment and request. While everything he or she promises really might fit into his or her job description, he or she cannot possibly do it all, and winds up disappointing someone who has asked for things the promiser says he or she will do but cannot deliver. Moreover, what he or she does do, the promiser usually does so rapidly because of time pressures that he or she does not do a first-rate job. Another—and perhaps worse—variant of the promiser is the boss who promises that his or her subordinates will deliver more than they possibly can. The promiser's acquiescence without regard to subordinates' existing commitments frequently does not allow them to set logical priorities, and it often shows that he or she lacks the skill to establish priorities. Such behavior also puts undue pressure on subordinates who may try to accomplish what the boss promises. If you fit into this category—particularly if you are making promises on behalf of your subordinates—try to step back and put things into perspective. Exercise control and incorporate good planning into your way of doing business. Promising too much is really worse than promising nothing. You win admiration temporarily, but it is short-lived when others realize you cannot deliver what you say you can.

THE PEST (DEPENDENT)

The "pest" is an obvious designation: one who simply will not let others alone. Sometimes the pest just bothers co-workers, annoying them, but not jeopardizing his or her own position unless complaints from the co-workers drift back to management. At other times—and this is more common—the pest bothers his or her boss. This type of person needs direction and reinforcement for every step of every task. He or she does not have the confidence or, at times, the intelligence, to make a decision and carry out a plan or a project. Every idea the pest has and every action the pest takes requires the knowledge and approval of a supervisor, and the manager finds this person at his or her door many times a day. If you are such a person, you are clearly wasting company time—your own, your manager's, your colleagues—and because of the nature of the offense, it is frequently not difficult for your employer to document incompetence on a performance review. If the pest-dependency goes on too long, you might find yourself on the job market, and people with this type of problem frequently have trouble hiding this characteristic at a job interview. Sometimes, if you are aware that you are this type of person, it is wise to begin taking the initiative on tasks and projects, and to attempt to work more independently before your dependency becomes too annoying to your boss.

THE PEST (SHOW-OFF)

Another kind of pest is the show-off, the person who must seek kudos for everything he or she does. This trait, too, can be extremely annoying to co-workers and to managers. Not only do they resent the constant demand to pat someone else on the back, but they also resent the fact that the show-off rarely returns anyone's compliments. If you are this kind of employee, look into yourself and see whether what you are seeking is corroboration that you are capable of doing your job. If a lack of confidence is your problem, it will not help your co-workers or your boss in dealing with you any more effectively, but it may help you understand what you are doing. Rather than wait until others find reasons to get rid of you, consciously try not to brag for a while. You might be surprised to find you elicit as much praise and reinforcement by not singing your own glory as by doing so.

THE SUPER-INDEPENDENT

On the other side of the spectrum is the super-independent—the person who never consults with anyone about anything. Not even this person's boss knows what he or she is up to. The real danger here is not the independence per se; if a person does a good job, independence is regarded as a fine characteristic. The real danger is that the person could be headed in a mistaken direction, often with dire business consequences. Such a person wastes personnel time, company money, and employer patience, and frequently messes things up badly enough to be fired on the spot. If you tend to be independent in this negative way, you might be covering up a lack of confidence; but if this is so, by the time you complete your "independent" work you might find yourself out of a job. Check in with your boss from time to time, to make sure you are on the right track; show interim results when appropriate; and don't hesitate to ask for guidance if you need it.

THE WISHY-WASHY WIMP

Another type of failure is the person who is so indecisive that he or she can never make a decision or stick to a plan. Any thought anyone else voices immediately causes him or her to abandon the most recently held point of view and adopt another. The result, of course, is that nothing ever gets done because no plan is ever carried through, and the projects this type of person works on have little credibility to others because the wishy-washy wimp is viewed by most as a nonentity. Many people who are successful in business are fairly aggressive, and someone who is not only nonaggressive but indecisive and shy is frequently walked over and ignored. If you are of this nature, you might be in the wrong field if you are in a competitive business area. Excessively shy and indecisive personalities are hard to shed because they are often deep-rooted. You could try to be more decisive and aggressive, but recommending that you effect a career change might be better advice. An extreme form of the wishy-washy wimp is the person who fails because he or she is so sure everyone is out to "get" him or her, that he or she is powerless to accomplish anything. He or she sees competitiveness in every move co-workers make, and also thinks the boss is just waiting to catch him or her making a mistake. So debilitating is the fear of reprisal and disaproval in this type of person that these fears become self-fulfilling prophecies, and the person can barely function at all. If you are this type of person, you may benefit from some sort of personality or career counseling.

THE ANACHRONISM

An "anachronism" is defined as a person or thing that is chronologically out of place. In the business world, it is the person who cannot help referring to—and by implication, preferring—the ways things used to be done twenty years ago, or the way things were done at the last job in the old company. While not all old ways of doing things are bad or even outdated and a certain degree of comparison and stocktaking is essential to an organization's effectiveness, employees who constantly live in the past or long for a bygone environment are a nuisance and a frustration to others, and are often so to themselves as well. Typically, they cannot adjust to change and cannot recognize changes in situations or environments which necessitate change.

Maurice Berkeley was such a person. He had been the editor of a corporate newsletter—a "house organ"—at a major insurance corporation for over fifteen years, and he had seen the field of corporate communications change radically during that time. The purpose of communications had evolved from an attempt to build cohesion among the various segments of a company's population, especially at the nonprofessional level, to an effort at communicating important business messages and strategic goals to the company's employees. Morale-building and solidarity were still important goals of communication, but these goals were seen to be more effectively achieved by telling employees what the company and the industry were doing, not by listing marriages and retirements or by printing photographs of smiling faces receiving twenty-five-year service pins.

Maurice had seen a number of communications managers come and go and viewed the shifts in communications policy that accompanied these changes with alarm and with an increasing tenacity to the old way of writing a company newspaper. He also had difficulty accepting the major changes that were taking place in the insurance industry—shifts in the kinds of business it did and services it provided, different marketing strategies and customer bases, and changing regulatory conditions—changes that communications managers wanted reflected in corporate publications. Maurice resisted all attempts to fit the publication to the times, excusing his refusal to alter his magazine with the fact that it had won prizes for writing and design in the past. He stubbornly rejected criticism, cajolery and other attempts to make him refine and update "his" publication, and eventually became a crotchety albatross. His management was reluctant to fire an employee who had put so much of his professional life into the company, and Maurice ignored all hints about a corporate transfer or early retirement. Instead, Maurice continued to work on his publication until the head of his department concocted a harmless "administrative advancement" for Maurice to fill his years until he was of mandatory retirement age—a corporate gratuity.

If you sense that you, yourself, are in a situation similar to Maurice's, it might be best to determine why you are becoming an anachronism and to take stock of your options. Are you old-fashioned because the advancements in your field have left you behind? If so, perhaps professional seminars or classes, or even a refresher course or two in your field at a university or business institute would help you keep your skills and understanding of the workplace up to date. Are you tired of the professional grind? Then maybe early retirement is the answer. Is your problem really a new management structure you simply do not relate to on a personal level? If this is the case, then maybe it is time to change departments or companies, even if your investment in years spent in the corporation is extensive.

THE MALICIOUS CO-WORKER

The last type of failure we shall note is the vicious and malicious co-worker. Jealousy and spite frequently prompt such a person to expose everyone else's failings and weaknesses, even if it takes a bit of lying to convince others that his or her malicious perceptions are valid. A subtly vicious person is especially dangerous because his or her true motives for spreading malice are often undetected. What finally undermines this type of person is usually the proverbial chickens coming home to roost. Enemies don't help you if you're down. There are many excusable types of weaknesses, but meanness isn't one of them, and if you are a truly vicious type of person, a thorough self-analysis might be in order.

Most of us may feel that we possess some of the above traits some of the time, but in our normal work experience, we learn to temper our shortcomings and to put up with those of others. We frequently learn what our weaknesses are by observing the reactions of those around us. An excess of one or more of the above traits can lead to a serious career problem. If you are perceptive enough to realize you have a personality problem that is leading you to professional failure, it is time to do some serious self-assessment. Perhaps repeated failure at a certain kind of job means that at some very basic level, despite your training and apparent skills, you are really not suited for the type of work you are doing. Think about changing careers; or make a parallel move to another department or line of work; or, more drastically but perhaps more sensibly, take a step downward. Succeeding at a lower level is at least more satisfying than repeatedly failing at a higher level.

Maureen Hanrahan did just that. In two years she had been removed from three different jobs in a company that hired her as a highly paid professional. First she was hired to work in the accounting office. When it was discovered that her mathematical skills were really not sufficient to handle the work, despite her "credentials," she was moved to the corporate communications area. She proved weak in writing and interpersonal skills and failed there, too; and she failed again in the human resources department to which she was next moved. Desperately afraid she would be fired from the company—a realistic fear since the company had been especially patient in trying to keep her—Maureen finally realized that she had only one really provable skill: she was excellent as a word processing operator. She swallowed her pride and accepted the company's final offer of a transfer to the secretarial pool. She functioned very well in her new position. Although her salary was cut, she found that she could still manage financially, and the satisfaction of having found a job she could do well more than made up for the hurt pride and belt-tightening. Her job success had an effect on her personality as well. She became less hostile and easier to work with. Within months she was promoted to word processing supervisor, a position of some authority which paid almost as much as the positions she had lost, and a position at which she could really succeed.

Another repeated failure was Rachel Joyner. Rachel made a succession of parallel moves between companies, each after eighteen months on the job and each after assuring herself that her failure to achieve a meteoric rise in the company was due to her manager's lack of appreciation for her talents. She thought each failure was an isolated case and she overlooked the fact that she couldn't get along with anyone. Moroever, she didn't recognize that she expected more than just the ordinary promotions and raises and became hostile when they weren't forthcoming. After her third dismissal, Rachel took stock of her situation and gave a critical look at the chances of her eventual success in a career. Without actually coming to grips with her abrasive personality, she did recognize that she worked better on her own than with a group, and decided to do something entrepreneurial.

This, in turn, posed an additional problem: she had not established enough contacts in her field to go out on her own and secure individual clients. So she, too, swallowed her pride and applied to her uncle for a position she knew he wanted to fill in his art business. He wanted someone to begin a small branch gallery which specialized in rare Oriental art. (His own large gallery specialized in European paintings.) He needed someone schooled in Oriental art and business, whose absolute honesty he could trust. His niece, who had an MBA in accounting and whose honesty he was sure of, fitted only two of his three criteria, but because of the family relationship, he was willing to hire her. He did insist that she undertake the study of Oriental art in her spare time. This approach would work out in terms of the timing of the business because he, himself, intended to be involved in the initial stages of the business.

Rachel knew she got the job through nepotism and was only partially qualified for it, but she also knew she would have the initiative to succeed because she was really interested in the project. The beginning salary was very low, but Rachel accepted this because she knew she had to prove herself, and because she had no other alternative. (She realized that getting other jobs like her previous ones would result in additional failures.) She also knew that if she succeeded in building up the business, her uncle would probably make her a partner. Being fairly young with no dependents, Rachel could afford to take a cut in salary. The end of the story was a happy one. Rachel's decisions here were solid ones, and she stuck to and succeeded in her original plans.

While Rachel's success depended in part on luck, many successful people appear to have had a lucky break at some time in their career. Often, a lucky break is no more than being astute enough to take advantage of an opportunity, minimal as it may appear at first, and work hard to make it succeed. Knowing your strengths and weaknesses, your ambitions and fears, what turns you on and what doesn't, is crucial to making the right career choice. And having the courage to begin at the beginning, even if it does not represent immediate high rewards, can pay off. Knowing when to hang on because you are building a future, and when to let go because you are on a dead end, is difficult, but essential, in building a career. Keeping your psyche intact and maintaining a sense of perspective—losing a job is not the end of the world—is also a key to eventual success. You can make strides in achieving success and overcoming failure if you are honest with yourself and introspective enough to determine what you can do well, and then go and do it.

Chapter 11
How Far You Can Go

In the final analysis, does success in the business staff world depend upon strategy or accident? A little bit of both, and a lot of something else, too—energy. A successful career in the business world—whether it is in a line or staff career path—needs a master plan. The standard question, "Where do you see yourself in five years?" is not an idle one on the part of most seasoned interviewers. They know that your answer to that question will reveal whether you know where your own career decisions might lead you, and whether you know what skills you must have and develop to get there. Your answer will also indicate just how serious you are about your career. A real commitment requires some long-range thinking.

Mapping out a career path, however, isn't something you simply sit down one day and do. It is an evolving process. You should constantly reassess your direction, your performance, your goals, and the realities of the economic world in which you are functioning. Although you should have a master plan, keep it flexible so that you can recognize unplanned opportunities and seize them, and so that you can alter your direction if you or the economy at large isn't moving as anticipated.

Everyone's success story really has an individual stamp, and yours will, too. There is no prescription for achievement. Your success, whether you are in a small firm or a large corporation, will depend on a number of obvious factors: your skills, motivation, and self-awareness; your boss and your relationship with him or her; the worth in the organization of your department or the worth to its clients of your firm; your competition; and the general economy. Being proactive and energetically pursuing career advancements also helps. Another factor is the ability to keep up with—or even ahead of—the times. Knowing when to learn new skills (before your old ones become obsolete) is of vital importance in this changing world.

How far you can go in a field, however, is not only dependent on your skills. It is also dependent on how far there is to go. Various areas and types of companies have different advancement potential. You should know what the highest levels of staff work consist of in your area, and you should be aware of the plateaus that exist along the way so that you can set your goals accordingly. You may hope to reach the top; you may aim for a place not as powerful or demanding; or you may decide to leave the level of your achievement to fate. You should know what there is to attain so you won't be surprised by what's up there when you climb high enough to get a good look around. You should know what each type of staff job can ultimately lead to so you can set realistic sights.

Corporate staff departments such as human resources, community affairs, administration, and corporate communications are usually structured in similar ways. Each department is headed by a high-level professional, who has usually worked his or her way up through the department (or a similar department in another organization), who controls that area's functions, and who serves as the liaison between the department and the corporate management, the department and other staff areas, and the department and the line area. The head of the department ordinarily reports to the chief administrative officer of the company, who might, himself or herself, have risen through the ranks of a staff department, or to the chief operating or executive officer of the company, who are ordinarily line people. See Figure 11-1.

These department-head positions are generally as far as staff workers can go in corporations, but they represent a very high level, both in terms of salaries—often in six figures—and in power and prestige. It is, of course, rare to achieve such cor-

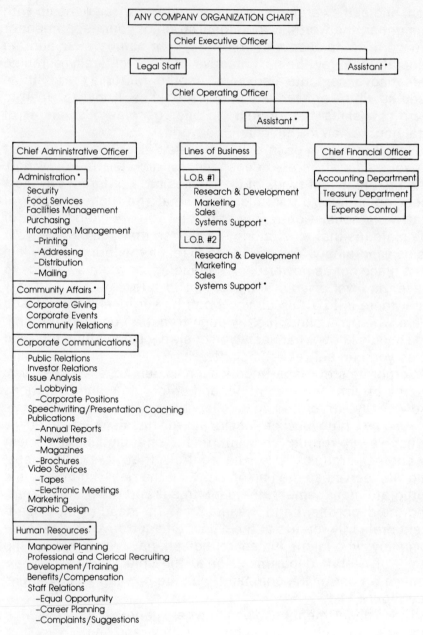

FIGURE 11-1   Staff Opportunities

porate heights—since dozens, or even hundreds, of professionals who rise to middle management in any given company may be competing for the same slot at any given time.

The department head manages a group of functions, each of which is also led by a fairly senior and powerful and well-paid professional. For example, the head of human resources might have reporting to him or her group heads of such areas as compensation, benefits, staff relations, professional and clerical recruiting, health services, and training and development.

Depending on the size of the organization, the groups might be divided into subspecialties, with each smaller unit headed by a fairly high-ranking professional as well. For instance, the training group might be divided into professional training, clerical training, and orientation, and might even have a group serving the needs of those who wish to study for a university or professional degree. The benefits group might be subdivided into units handling health care, dental care, profit sharing, etc. Moreover, in very large organizations, even project-head positions are highly paid and prestigious. Each of these leadership positions can be a plateau for a staff professional—a goal, an achievement, a position passed through on the way to achieving something even better. The limit to advancement in human resources work is at a very high level.

One human resources success was George Carpenter. He was a history major at a "Big Ten" university in the midwest. He played football, although he wasn't the brightest star on the team, and he got reasonable grades. By the middle of his senior year he was convinced that he didn't want to do what most of his classmates were doing: he had no outstanding special skills, so he couldn't consider professional sports or music, etc.; he had no special interest in teaching or research, so graduate school in an academic subject was out; he didn't want to be a lawyer or a health services specialist, so he dismissed professional schools; taking a chance on getting a generalist, entry-level job at any old corporation and working his way up didn't have any appeal; and the financial jobs most MBAs landed were uninteresting to him as well.

He was feeling a bit lost until he talked to a placement counselor at his university who suggested taking a business school degree in human resources and going into the field of personnel. He balked at first, thinking "personnel" meant only interviewing clerical applicants, but became interested upon hearing about the other types of positions for which a human resources degree would enable him to apply.

George applied to and was accepted for a flexible MBA program in New York where he specialized in the compensation and benefits area. He also found that, although math had never been his strongest subject, the finance and accounting courses he had to take as part of his program were not only interesting, but obviously useful as a basis for studying compensation and benefits planning, and not as difficult as he had imagined they would be.

Two years later, degree in hand, George became a member of the compensation-and-benefits team at a small electronics concern in Philadelphia. Because the corporation was small, George was given a lot of responsibility in a fairly short time. Because of unusual turnover in his department, it took him just a bit more than five years to rise several levels to department head, and then he was hired away by a major financial services firm in New York City—a parallel move in terms of job function (he was still head of compensation and benefits), but a significant increase in terms of the size of the organization and the size of his salary. Six years later, after successfully and imaginatively leading his department, he was again recruited by an enterprising headhunter for a position as head of all of personnel functions for a major international conglomerate. At the age of thirty-five, he had a prestigious position of considerable influence in a world-reknowned conglomerate, with an accompanying six-figure salary and a good crack at the senior management levels of his company within a few years.

George moved faster and further than most in his area because he was very good at his job and was willing to work hard. He focused his energies and imaginative abilities on doing the best for his employer, and it paid off. Luck and timing were also on his side. For him, the staff world was a natural way to the top.

Similar opportunities exist in the community affairs and administration areas, and in corporate communications. There is usually a director of the entire department, then group heads, and within these groups there is even further breakdown. To be head of any of these areas might be considered a very respectable professional goal.

One success story from such a staff area involves Anita Redford. A line banker, credit-trained, with an MBA behind her, Anita was plodding along at a rate equal to that of the other lending officers at the large Boston bank in which she worked. Taking advantage of the fact that the bank's new management seemed to encourage women to advance to higher positions, she accepted an offer to lead the organization's small London office, hoping by this widening of her experience to single herself out from her peers. She did a creditable and imaginative job in London, but her real opportunity came from an unexpected quarter: the staff world. her bank was having trouble managing the administrative services department—the area which oversees certain building facilities and service functions. The long-time head of the department died suddenly, and his temporary replacement, formerly his second-in-command, was clearly not competent to run the area. Functions were breaking down, good people were leaving the department, and complaints were coming in from all over the bank about how bad the services and facilities were becoming. There were no managers within the administrative services department whose experience level warranted catapulting them to the head of the area, and besides, the bank's senior management thought it would be useful to bring in a manager from an area which had a history of being tightly run. They also thought someone from another area—particularly a line area—would have fresh ideas about how to organize the department for maximum efficiency.

When they approached Anita about the job, her first reaction was to shun it because it was a staff position, and she "knew" the way to the top was to stay on the line. But when they offered her a senior vice presidency, and a much higher salary as well, she found it was an offer she couldn't refuse. They also said she could return to a line position at a later time, though she wondered if they meant it. She returned to Boston, full of anxiety about whether she had boxed herself into a position with no future, but also eager to prove herself in a rather challenging situation.

She found the job much to her liking. The people were just as sharp as those she had left "on the line," and were more friendly and relaxed than her former colleagues. She plunged right in, and in two years, through a mixture of toughness and dedication, she had turned the department into a well-organized, productive, and efficient machine. She was just beginning to think that she would be perfectly happy even if this were the highest level she ever attained when the bank's senior management made good on their original promise and offered her an opportunity to become the bank's first female senior vice president in a line area.

Although Anita's staff experience took place at a fairly high level, many other success stories about line career paths involve experience at one time or another in a staff group.

In some corporations—particularly ones with very technical business lines—the heads of staff divisions are routinely drawn from the line; but in others, working one's way up through a department is the accepted route.

The same kinds of staff opportunities exist in small firms as in large corporations. The organization of a small firm differs markedly from that of a big company, but the money and the prestige are present in both. The structure of a small firm— whether marketing human resources or communications or other consulting services—is likely to consist of several project managers and a smaller number of senior partners who drum up the business, direct the project managers, and split the profits. The structure of a small firm might look like this:

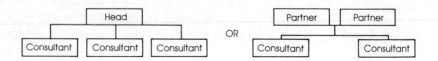

Working in a small firm or large corporation can each have advantages in terms of getting ahead. Both offer fairly high-level positions and good salaries. The difference is really one of personal taste. If there are any generalizations to be made, it might be said that there is more prestige to be had from being the head of a large department in a corporation than there is from heading a small firm, because you are generally managing more people; but it can also be said that there is a possibility of making more money working as the head of a small firm than in a large company. Some people find that at different times during their career, one or the other will suit their needs better. Two examples will illustrate this.

Robert Romano and Ted Bronson followed career paths in reverse directions. Robert began his career with a decision to teach English at the university level. He received his Ph.D. in Victorian literature, but when it came time to look for a position, the poor job market for college teachers, small salaries they offered, and the fact that Robert was disenchanted with teaching after an experience as a teaching assistant during graduate school combined to cause him to set his career direction on another course. He spent a few years as a writer on a bank publication, then decided to go out on his own as a communications consultant.

He knew that building up a client base would be slow going, but he was young, ambitious, worked hard, and had no children to support. In addition, he had a wife with a steady income from a well-paying professional position, so he could afford a slow start. He began his search for a clientele with those communicators with whom he had worked at the bank. They were familiar with his work, so they were not reluctant to give him free-lance writing assignments from time to time. He also kept up with those of his former academic colleagues who were in professional communications jobs. In many cases, they were happy to give him assignments because he provided more than many free-lancers provided: he was very thorough and analytical in researching and structuring material as a result of his academic studies; he was a very facile writer; and his rates were low.

Robert's business began to increase, and although he wasn't

getting rich, he was earning his bread and butter. A lucky break came when one of his former clients from the bank moved to a major electronics firm and was given the responsibility of setting up an entire communications department. He called on Robert for help, and this began a client relationship for Robert which involved work in everything from communications planning—setting up publications and programs—to speech writing and video production.

Robert soon had more work than he could handle, and as the relationship looked pretty permanent—the electronics communications manager liked the flexibility of dealing with freelance help—he decided to set up his own small firm and hire a staff. He moved into quarters owned by a design firm, which was a convenient relationship for designing print material he was working on, and eventually developed his business into a thriving medium-sized firm. His company's contacts and reputation increased with his income, and soon he numbered several major corporations among his steady clientele.

Ted Bronson moved in the reverse direction. He began his career with a small group of public relations consultants. He had worked on his college newspaper and had been bitten by the journalism bug, but he was not willing to relocate to an area outside a metropolitan center and job opportunities for a rookie reporter in cities were slim. He knew a partner in a medium-size New York PR firm, and landed an entry-level job establishing press contacts for a large conglomerate client of the firm.

Ted worked hard, becoming an assistant manager, then account manager after several years. He still dealt with the press, but his responsibilities increased to include writing press releases and other promotional products, and a host of other duties. He found dealing with clients very easy, since he was extremely personable and articulate and had no trouble selling his services, and decided that since he was young and unattached in a personal sense, he would go out on his own and establish a business.

The first years were rough, being recession years, and Ted thought several times of giving up and going back to working for an established PR firm. He stuck it out, however, and as the economy started to improve, so did his business. His clients, although they took a lot of work to attract initially, were pleased with Ted's personal, thorough, and consistent attention to their public relations needs and stuck with his firm, even though it was a fledgling operation. His most prestigious client was a major financial institution, which gave him several assignments. During a period of crisis, the institution felt that it was imperative that they have a person like Ted on staff permanently, and asked him to join them full time.

It was a rough decision to leave the firm he had worked so hard to establish, but Ted saw more security, guaranteed income, and stability in working for a large institution; besides, he would be coming in at a very senior level. He accepted the offer and joined the company. After helping them turn around during the crisis period, he became a trusted advisor of senior management; established a large and productive department; and attained the rank of executive vice president and head of all staff groups.

Ted wondered if he would regret losing his independence as the head of a firm. He didn't. His hours, though long, were generally more predictable than they were before, and he didn't have the anxiety of wondering whether his clients would suddenly disappear. Moreover, he really enjoyed being part of the company that was, in reality, very central to the success of the world's economy.

Now near the mandatory corporate retirement age, Ted is contemplating working independently again, but this time there will be no financial sacrifice, since his corporate pension will enable him to live comfortably even if his efforts at establishing another clientele fail.

Becoming a group, division, or department head is not the only way to rise in a corporate environment. Assistant-to jobs are often positions of power, prestige, and high monetary reward, and such positions rarely involve managing a staff or even projects. Being privy to the highest levels of corporate decision-making or being the power behind the throne can be ends in themselves. And it should not be forgotten that a position as assistant to the chief gives one a tremendous amount of exposure and allows one a great deal of flexibility. One major advantage is that the holder of such a position becomes knowledgeable about all phases of the corporation's business, and thus is a prime candidate for a senior management slot.

An assistant-to who climbed to the top was Charles Berkeley. He began his communications career by enlisting in the army. He didn't really think Uncle Sam was looking for people who liked to write, but he thought he'd give Uncle Sam the opportunity of making use of someone who had good communications skills. Boot camp didn't seem to be a particularly good match with his writing capabilities, but Charles did eventually wind up doing communications for the army. He wrote public relations releases.

When he was discharged from the service, he parlayed his experience into a professional-level job in the PR department of a major midwestern food company. He wrote news releases and position papers for the press and prepared speeches for some of the senior managers of his firm. He worked in this capacity for several years, receiving small promotions, and after a time was the head of a staff of four.

Charles's big break came when the company's president retired and a new president was appointed. Charles had written speeches for this individual, with whom he got along very well. The new president asked Charles to be his special assistant, a horse-holder position with the accompanying temptation of a vice president title.

Charles functioned very well in his new position, being blessed with a large degree of patience and a fairly laidback personality. He made some very good decisions, was rewarded with a large amount of responsibility, received a wide variety of projects and assignments, and worked closely with the firm's entire senior management team. After three years in this position, the company's public relations and communications director—a senior vice president with strategic planning responsibilities—left the company, and the president could think of no one more well-suited to the job or more familiar with the organization than Charles. So, in just a few years—and lots of hard work—Charles went from army private to highly paid corporate executive, achieving his goals through the most persistent use of his talents.

It is clear from considering staff career paths that the top of the line in corporations is department head, or occasionally (for superstars) the senior reaches of management; in small firms, partner or head. And it is apparent that a talented aide-de-camp can also parley his or her position into a senior-level job. But what about those performing a staff function in a line department, such as a marketing or research person in a business unit? Usually, the heads of line business areas are those with customer contact and experience in developing and selling the product produced. It is generally assumed that only a person with experience on the business side knows the area enough to run it; and a staff person's highest goal in most cases such as this is managing the function in which he or she works.

However, there are exceptions to this generality. If your staff position includes working closely with the line-of-business people, especially at the top, and if your experience includes customer contact, there is a possibility that you can be one of these exceptions. If your work is highly visible to the department manager and if he or she thinks it is valuable to the firm, if you have demonstrated managerial skills, and if your technical knowledge is sufficient to handle the business of the department, you might be in a position to be seriously considered for a line management job.

If by observing the activities going on around you in a line department you are convinced that you can do this work and you would like to pursue a line career, be sure to indicate your interest in doing so to your department head. Frequently, staff people are overlooked for promotion to jobs they could easily handle because no one knows they have an interest in trying a line position. If you talk to your boss or the area head about your ambitions, you will quickly find out whether they feel your experience is sufficient, whether you need more training, or whether they feel you are totally unsuited to such a career path. If the latter case is true for you, you are better off learning early that you are not perceived as a line person so that you can make your career plans accordingly, either by concentrating on staff work or by pursuing your ambitions elsewhere. If you need more training, you might begin to take courses and seminars in your spare time while performing a staff function; and you also might consider taking a step downwards to an entry-level line position if you are really committed to switching to the line.

If you are a member of a technical staff department—systems, accounting, or legal—your potential to rise to the top of your area depends on your technical or professional skills, just as it does in communications and human resources departments. Technical experts can frequently get pretty far. However, few systems officers or accountants become CEOs of firms that do not specialize in systems or accounting. More often, a lawyer may rise to a senior position within a corporation, even if it is not a law firm. For example, there are several very high-level executives at major commercial banks who began their careers as lawyers.

To sum up, the answer to the question of how far you can go as a staffer in a line world is: right to the top, in terms of money, prestige, power, and visibility. Like everything in life, the variation is large. If your technical, interpersonal, and analytical skills are high, and if you make the best of the opportunities that come your way, and—yes—if you are lucky enough to be in the right place at the right time, you can become a superstar. But even if you don't climb to the corporate ladder's top—if you choose to stay or wind up on a rung lower down, you can still get professional satisfaction and concrete rewards from a staff job. You can achieve a high degree of professionalism and stability, and secure a job with a future.

For many, the business staff world is an interesting alternative to line jobs and to careers in nonprofit organizations. Many staff jobs require a high degree of professionalism, and the rewards and satisfactions can be commensurate with the effort put forth. The staff world may be the right place for you.

Conclusion

The purpose of this book hasn't been to convince you to pick a career path in the staff world, or to encourage you to pursue goals in the line areas, but to enable you to determine what is best for you and how to succeed in the area you have chosen. These are some lessons in the book from which all professionals can benefit:

- Be self-aware about your needs and talents.
- Know what professional goals you want to achieve, or at least how to go about figuring them out.
- Maximize your strengths and learn to overcome your weaknesses.
- Be confident about your abilities, but also be realistic about your limitations.
- Know when to proceed and when not to.
- Think long-range as well as short-range, and develop strategies for your career.
- Don't let failure get you down. Use the experience to reassess your goals.
- Learn from your own experience and from that of others.
- Have the energy and determination to *try* to succeed.

There is also one lesson implicit in this book that should stand out from all the rest: Don't measure "success" in terms of money, power, or prestige, but rather in terms of personal fulfillment. This lesson has been well-stated by an old man, a retired business executive—not a CEO, but close—in a remark to a friend. He said:

In my career, I tried for big successes. I got some; I didn't get others. But in looking back, the "biggest" successes and disappointments didn't make or break my career; nor did they make me feel the best or the worst. Some of the most meaningful successes to me were actually little accomplishments when seen against the whole picture; they were often ones that nobody else even noticed. And my most disturbing failure wasn't that I never got to the *very* top, but that when I got near the top, I was competing with an old friend and colleague for the position. Getting the job cost me his friendship, and that's one of my deepest regrets. It's really the little things—often gotten serendipitously—that count the most and that make a career.

Keep this in mind when pursuing your goals, and good luck in your career.

Index

190

To order,

contact your local bookstore, or send the order form to

Scott, Foresman and Company

Professional Publishing Group
1900 East Lake Avenue
Glenview, IL 60025

In Canada, contact

Macmillan of Canada
164 Commander Blvd.
Agincourt, Ontario
M1S 3C7

Please check method of payment:

☐ Check/Money Order   ☐ MasterCard   ☐ Visa

Amount Enclosed $_____

Credit Card No. _____

Expiration Date_____

Signature _____

Name (please print)_____

Address_____

City _____ State _____ Zip _____

Add applicable sales tax, plus 6% of Total for U.P.S.
Full payment must accompany your order. Offer good in U.S. only.

A18087